ASHES AND SEEDS

Michelle Greenblatt

Unlikely Books
www.UnlikelyStories.org
New Orleans, Louisiana

ASHES AND SEEDS
Copyright © 2014 Michelle Greenblatt
Front Cover from "Ophelia" Copyright © Stephen Harrison
Back Cover from "Der Trauerflor der weißen Frau" Copyright © Monika Mori | MOO
Book and Cover Design Copyright © 2014 Unlikely Books

All Rights Reserved

ISBN-13: 978-0-9907604-2-9

Unlikely Books
www.UnlikelyStories.org
New Orleans, Louisiana

ASHES AND SEEDS

The Order in Which They Appear

Introduction by Jonathan Penton	9
Part I: Chapters of Absence	15
Streaks of Scarlet: A Story in 100 Parts	17
Part II: Except for Then	49
No Alembic	51
Precipice and Periphery	52
Catherine's Absence	54
Atomic time.	56
Songs of Elemental Change	60
Half-life.	61
Yours Now	62
The Names of the Dead	63
Terrible Fires	65
Call My Name, I'll Bring the Rain	66
Shadows Turn Bright	67
I Am Blackness Walking	68
The (W)hole of the Unknown	69
Burning Leaves in Hollywood Hills Park	71
From the Shadowside.	72
A Silver Sliver of Moon	73
Nicotine and Time	74
No Metronome	76
Salt	78
My Light with Your Teeth	79
Operatic Blurrings	80
About Tenses	81

How We Died, All Those Times   82
The Name I Once Went By   84
Beginning with Distance   85
Pound and Flutter   86
Hypothermic Silence   87
Committment above All   88
Corpus Delicti   89
The Cartographer's Diagnostics   90
Snake in the Grass   91
Let There Be Thorns   92
Novocain   94
Subject and Icon   95
Formerly Enchanted   97
Ante-Mortem   99
Except for Then   101

Part III: The Perpetual Principles of a Dream   103
The cage-dance.   105
Exsanguination.   107
Against the grey.   108
Almost liquid.   109
Tiniest, final perfection.   110
The smallest of sighs.   111
Calling down an avalanche.   112
The day you carved me into concentric circles.   113
Ice blossoms on the snowfield.   114
Struggle and flight.   115
Six years into my posthumous life.   116
A *posteriori*.   117
The question of thrown stones.   118
Stone among stones.   119

Imagelines.	120
Water's desolate edge.	121
Filled with winter.	122
A sufficient distance.	123
Mo(u)rning announcements.	124
Color of crying.	125
Intent on haphazardness.	126
Missing.	127
Press through panic.	128
Midnight and mud.	129
Clotted wisdom.	130
Employ then empty.	131
And *how does that make you feel?*	132
Softly, softly.	133
After the holocaust.	134
Highlighter fluid and water.	135
All life's discolorations.	136
Steel smiles in time.	137
The splitting tissues of time.	138
Persephone's blood.	139
Almost April.	140
Burns another spoon.	141
Darkening the West.	142
Shorn-blue.	143
Code red.	144
Self-division.	145
He fell away.	146
Celestial utterances.	147
Where you will find us.	148
Pitch.	149
Mouth to skin.	150

On black limbs.	151
Consecrated.	152
Repairing the black.	153
Each perceptual pause.	154
Without the help of a ladder.	155

Acknowledgements 157
About the Author 159

Publisher's Introduction

If you read books on the history of 20th Century poetry (stay with me folks, it's something that some people do), whether written at the time or since, you'll find a broad desire to avoid discussing the Confessional movement. This is remarkable, because while the Beats might've been the literary movement to become (justly or otherwise) synonymous with inevitable cultural change, Confessional poetry is synonymous with the inevitable democratization of poetry: the spread of the personal poem that proliferated with the rise of the photocopier and reached maturity on the Internet.

The term "Confessional" is inherently vague, which might account for some of the critical quiet. First used by M. L. Rosenthal in 1959 to describe the works of Robert Lowell, the term describes poetry that has a therapeutic purpose, for the author, in the writing, and typically, but not necessarily, relies heavily on the "I" word. Such a literary philosophy long predates 1959—I'll argue that it includes most novels and all myth. Still, Lowell readily attached himself to the descriptor, associating it with literature's natural changes in subject matter as American culture, confused about gender and terrified of technology, fractured. Confessional poetry became associated with psychosexual contemplations, solidifying into an emotional and "romantic" counterpoint to the open sexuality of the Beats and Hippies. Traditionally, women are more interested in such contemplations than men, and when two of Lowell's students, Sylvia Plath and Anne Sexton, became associated with the term, the jargon, illogically, solidified further: Confessional poetry became the poetry of not only women, but girls. If a non-poet knows the term "Confessional poetry," they very likely associate it with teenage girls. Thus might some of the term's relative critical obscurity be described: *no one* wants to be a teenage girl.

This near-universal truth might be described as sexism, but it is not, itself, misogyny: it's common sense. Girlhood, as this book makes clear, is dangerous and unhealthy. No sane person would ever want to be a teenage girl. Teenage girls live in circumstances which make sanity nearly impossible, but even when they are raised to be sane and can remain so, they exist in a state of constant physical and psychic peril. "Misogyny" can be defined as the way in which we are so ready to blame girls for their terrifying existence, and while our culture's omnipresent misogyny is reprehensible, it is not actually surprising. Girlhood is a trauma so complete, yet so pervasive, that we are all forced to revisit it constantly. We do this with legitimate film and literature, but also passively, in every news report, in every advertisement, in every song and music video. The male who avoids reflecting on girlhood is perpetually assaulted by reminders of it, in a way that inevitably causes irrational response. Thus, misogyny (along with a fixation on youth) deepens and girlhood becomes more dangerous, creating a cycle that would threaten our species were there not so many cultural voices ready to combat it.

Such is the context in which the term Confessionalism is typically used or avoided, and such is the context of *ASHES AND SEEDS*. The book is, quite openly, a therapeutic exploration of the author's girlhood. Unlikely Books, and its parent, the electronic magazine *UnlikelyStories.org*, has published a number of works on this topic. In several ways, *ASHES AND SEEDS* is the most traditional of these. The psychosexual relationships described here are essentially heteronormative. Gender and sexuality are not particularly experimental; the book is not overtly feminist (although it is obviously the product of an author who understands and appreciates feminist discourse). The poetic forms used are often quite contemporary, particularly the haibun: a combination of prose poem and haiku that, in its English-language incarnation, is very 21st Century, and collaged here with quotes from literature and pop lyrics. But the greater structure of the book is narrative: its three sections build an emotional autobiography in the manner of Lowell's books—that is, in a 20th Century way. It is therapy, and it is storytelling: it is a straightforward attempt to share the author's trauma in a way that allows the reader to examine their own.

Michelle's choice of structure is particularly interesting given her age, and the technological and literary context in which she left girlhood. Born in 1982, she was a teenager when Internet literature became a serious phenomenon: *UnlikelyStories.org* was founded before her sixteenth birthday. She did not spend a moment of her adult life contemplating whether or not the Internet was worthy of her poems: it was widely considered a legitimate venue for publication before she had any adult works to publish. Good literature responds to the technology that surrounds it, and Michelle has created many fine works and collaborations that could not easily exist outside of our era, working in visual poetry and other digitally-dependent forms. (Even so, there have always been things about her work that were out-of-step with the Age of Memes: consider her dedication to dating her drafts, and publishing this information, a concept that seems antithetical to much Internet publishing, in which entire books, sometimes quite deliberately, completely disappear overnight.) Here, though, the intent is not experimental, but mythological. Like Anne Sexton, Michelle "lie[s] a lot" when offering direct descriptions of events: the autobiographical nature of this book is symbolic. Unlike Sexton, Michelle rarely uses the word "I."

I suggest that all myths, from Anansi to Spider-Man, begin with an individual's attempt to describe their own existence in a universal (or at least very broad) way. Myths, after all, are guides and lessons. They might not be *moral* lessons, but they serve some instructional purpose: they describe life in an *applicable* way. Confessional poetry shares this intention, and the contemporary literary movements that reject Confessionalism tend to eschew, deliberately or otherwise, applicability: they sacrifice an author-reader connection in pursuit of beauty. In ASHES AND SEEDS, the context of the mythological lesson is very deliberate, and intertwined with Michelle's choices in form. The central character that guides ASHES AND SEEDS is clearly an autobiographical construct, but she is not "I," but "she:" a named figure that changes coloration and identity, as both Everywoman and Other. She lives in a castle, in a mythical garden, at the origins of the universe—whether or not she simultaneously lives in Florida.

But make no mistake: this book is neither sermon nor lecture. There is no suggestion, in ASHES AND SEEDS, that people can, by behaving in a correct way, experience positive results: quite the opposite. Most clearly, the book says that *girls suffer*, but beyond that, do not look for predictable outcomes. Rather, look for direct experience, honest analysis of the experience, and the wisdom that

Michelle Greenblatt

can come from such self-study. Michelle, in a truly Confessional work, has chosen the forms, techniques, and symbols that most authentically (if not always literally) tell the story of her vanishing girlhood. Through this, we readers hope to absorb a piece of her experience, and learn lessons that cannot make us safe, but might make us stronger.

—Jonathan Penton

for the man who loves me the most

Part I: Chapters of Absence

Streaks of Scarlet:
A Story in 100 Parts

for Kyle: one breath at a time

"Poor painted queen . . .
Why strew'st thou sugar on that bottled spider
Whose deadly web ensnareth thee about?
Fool, fool, thou whet'st a knife to kill thyself

Shakespeare
Richard III
Act I, Scene iii, ll. 239-242

Streaks of Scarlet: A Story in 100 Parts

1.
It's 7:13 p.m., she notes. She's just about to leave her cursed computer when another damned idea demands it's time / to bleed the screen again.

2.
I will come back...she starts, then pounds the delete key in fury. She hikes out to meet her edges.

3.
The motion of her eyelashes distracts her as she types, as does the defining urge to call this her autobiography. She considers this / sentence; she (re)considers herself. She looks out the window into the nothingness that envelops her. Having endured so many circular, identical events, how can she tell this story again?

4.
He drives a new, shiny-white BMW, which he now can't afford; he rides around all day, looking to score. He knows his cleverness is a weapon. *pour to melt*, he insists.

5.
She floats in a perpetual state of emulsion, strips the last bit of syntax that makes any sense into pieces that suit her purpose.

6.
Her hand speaks out loud as it slaps her
face repeatedly,
factually and with a plethora of brutalized dreams.

7.
She picks roses |cut| She picks skulls |cut| She picks perpetuation |cut|cut|cut|

8.
Only when the torment   of starvation   judges feeding   unavoidable does she finally   acquiesce, for the constant ache   of hunger is, on virtually any other day, preferable by   far to capitulating   (however briefly)   to the hollow

-eyed fates   of the others, those composed   almost entirely of bone, the scarce remnants of their stringy hair hanging   over the thin, translucent layers   of exhaustion   embedded in their eyes   and skin   wreathed in worms,

or those whose wrecked   flesh turned   to ash that went swirling forever   away on the whims   of a grey wind.

9.
She runs through the chalk hallways, the white pages, the chapters of absence, looking for anybody, anybody at all who knows her name.

10.
She crosses the arches of his palace gates with ease. Who knows him (and therefore his fortresses) better than she? Nobody. Nobody.

Even so, she is eventually detected and detained. Seeing no other way out of her imprisonment, she grits her teeth and bats her eyelashes, trying not to let the rage cloud her blue

eyes, shot

through with streaks of electric yellow / lightning. She carries no other currency than her body. Naked and terrified, she commits her briberies. Teeth clenched, she tells herself again and again she won't cry: she is fucking for the prince; he might even be pleased. As the guards take their pleasure (and little chinks of her fall away), they plot to betray her. They wait for the queen.

*

who is she? they whisper after they have taken (their turns with) her. They don't imagine she can hear them. None can match her features in any royal database. Facial recognition informs them she does not exist. They contact the FBI.

In hushed tones, they whisper, *how can we best be rid of her?* And: *is she dead because her eyes have gone black.*

11.
Shadows dance like firelight against the cold
stone walls.

She has lost the battle, fighting her self / hatred, and so it has crowded out the light. Now she will spread

only darkness for them.

12.
A memory: He won't wake up and she wants him to wake up. She repeats this to herself. *you won't wake up and I want you to wake up. you won't wake up and I want you to wake up, wake up, WAKE UP.* Each time she thinks this, she grows mightier

in her anger. She pauses, then rises, casting furious shadows onto the mirrorwalls.

13.
He is flecks of liquid placebo. He harbors his many hands inside her.

14.
disentangle! disentangle! she screams as she dashes through the palace corridors.

15.
witch
and *lunatic*, they murmur, shaking
their heads.

16.
Meanwhile, the prince is in the forest, hunting

butterflies. He catches them, scratches their feathers off. By this he means *oh, look what's left*. And: *here comes the butcher*. He does, of course, need to eat. And he can't fry those jeweled fish forever.

17.
His tongue is made of moonlight, of magic, of dreamlies. When she kissed him the first time—nearly nine years ago now—everything paused as her wish
(*let it always be this way, let it always be this beautiful*)
morphed to a smashing of prayers, then scattered into whispers—and the echoes of starless whirlwinds carried them away.

18.
(But his kisses were dust.)

19.
Stillness. A blackbird. All is silent in that bloodforest but for the sighs of the carbon-trees and the scrape scrape of butterfly wings as the prince performs their ritual slaughter for his feast.

20.
Road reverse, reverse road: she can't get away from this palace.

21.
The sky underfoot, the sun in her / skin (again, and always), skein of fire sweeping through her veins, blossoming in her gut, propelling her perpetually forward.

*

The foreground flies alongside her, colors blurring together in a haze of green and brown mingled with streaks of scarlet in the bloodsap leaking from the deviltrees. As for any context or sense of direction—she lost that long ago, when the weight of light broke her

back. Nothing but loneliness to keep her company now.

|cut|

*

begin, she thinks, begging herself to believe. *I must begin again.*

|cut|

*

But here comes the wall of sepulchral silence slamming into her. Her 6½ sapphires spill into the abyss.

|cut||cut||cut|

22.
The crank goes round: he's lost

and found

as the poison crosses his blood-brain

barrier. He glides, he soars, he smiles.

23.
A waterfall of phantoms gather in brief anonymous fields of filth, half-flattened prairie-grass, and other bleak deserted lots. The serpent that once gave her the best advice (*here is his love: hold it, keep holding...*) now surpasses the genius of his previously imparted wisdom with this new but ancient lesson:

he strikes at her, fangs sinking deep. He seems to shrug as he slithers away.

24.
Numb

-lipped, she sucks the poison from her veins. Heartsore and battered, she scrapes the burning dust of the alkali flowers from her skin and walks on: one step forward, one step back. *A girl needs a gun these days on account of the rattlesnakes*, she sings, laughing hysterically between syllables. She thinks of her prince, of the impossibility of rescue. She pictures her inevitable beheading.

*

The prince silences his rattler as he makes his stealthy escape. He is pleased with himself; the taste of her (blood) in his mouth—the intoxicating venom of betrayal.

25.
To Scarlet, the suicide pact they made at the beginning seems reasonable now—easy, even. She can tell by the bottle of benzodiazepines in her hand, by the crimson canteen she is filling with river-water. She fingers the razor in her pocket, notes the bulge of her veins, the twitch of her fingertips, her chattering teeth.

*

He watches his small scars and track marks flex and roll as he clenches and unclenches his fist, veins under the strain of the tourniquet. He doesn't hesitate: he capitulates to the sinking honeyburnt bliss.

26.
They made the pact when she was 13 and he was 15, both old / enough to know better, but they knew nothing

except themselves. Entrenched in the middle of a dark copse, the leaves filtered the silver moonlight pouring in: shimmering slantlight dancing with the shadows. Their tongues gave up kissing to the gravity of their promise; their fear bled into gradual day.

27.
it's okay, he whispers. *we can do it any time. any day. any way.*

28.
did you exist ever did you—Scarlet reaches for his hand, gone for so long now. But he left her a gift of slain sky, shredded narrower than her small despairing sighs.

29.
They must have collapsed on the moist ground, but the (lack of) hospital records contradicted the *corpus delicti*: blood and flesh / evidence they left on the forest floor.

30.
Though the queen has threatened beheading if Scarlet ever finds the prince, she has always been able to convince herself that opposition to violence and methodical revelation of truths will be enough to keep the blade away...

Always, until today.

31.
not true, not true, chants the prince. He is in 15 year-old form, laughing. Laughing. *because you forget that you forgot,* he whispers, but he's wrong. She hasn't forgotten anything.

32.
Her appetite outrages him; he pummels her face and chest, pounding her with his right fist, raking the nails of his left hand down her breast.

Nobody shapes their weapons like he.

33.
Rage taps on the window. The window taps on the door.

34.
She washes her hands in the river-blood. Wisps of her climb into the bus that runs back to the forest branching beyond the palace. She can't find a single place to pray amidst this, his vast darkling forest.

35.
where are you going? she asks him, because he won't come with her. He doesn't answer—he *never* answers. His image enlarges until the excruciating weight of him crushes her. He leaves her fresh as freesias

pressed between the pages of a forgotten photograph album.

36.
He gets in his BMW with the dead again, and scores.

37.
The prince's girlfriend shot

up in the passenger seat of his car. The girlfriend's sister wanted to play. But when little Shannon had a brain hemorrhage, nobody bothered to call *checkmate*. They still play the corpse game: driving, always driving. Their plaster(ed), smiling faces never change / expressions.

38.
don't be afraid, he says to Scarlet, *I can see you in the deathmirror.*

39.
what does this mean? she asks him.

40.
Greet the dead the way the dead greet you, she has learned

the hard way. He grabs her by the throat; he hides inside her / bones. She forgets what hands are for. *a light will come*, he promises her, *you will be held up and you will be blessed; you will be raised above the most glorious of altars.*

It is then that she remembers: *hands are for offering him needles.*

41.
O sand O silk O galactic black wild—she dances naked, breathless, on the web-spread surfaces of Zodiacal light.

O exposed bruises, O love doubled into madness, madness into self murder

flood of sunlight bouncing off dust particles, ions in the coronal plasma, forbidden spectral emission lines—

She reads pages of blank verse; her eyes skim the skies, registering the empty majestic light of heavenly bodies, most of which have already died; their light is an echo, a ghost chased by time.

She's drowning in the cold
moonlight.

42.
It's not the same, the hike through the mountains this day as it was at 1 a.m. on November 22, 1999. What she remembers best is *not* that forcefuck

against the concrete wall of darkness. What stays with her most of all is his cataclysmic act of banishment, delivered by the lips of another. The strong, unwanted man came

later (just as her prince's repentance did)...but "later" was far too late for her. He'd thrown her in the sepulchre, with the rest of the rotting bodies. In the morning, he realized

his mistake. He ran, red hair framing the dread / funereal sky. He flung himself against the stone door. *I'm sorry*, he whispered, *I was afraid. But I don't want to be alone. I want*

to be with you. He laid her (body) on the grass under the shade of a Cercis tree. She was cold, so cold...but she was breathing. He laughed, he cried, he held her to him. Even then,

he didn't notice something was wrong. *it's alright,* he told her, *it's okay. here we are, together again, and we'll try...we'll try to lead another life—a better life—and we'll succeed. you'll see.*

Which of them had cried then, a single tear dripping down a pale, frightened cheek? It didn't matter. By the time he'd come back for her, he was too late.

All those hours spent with rotting bodies—
—by then she thought she was dead again.

43.
don't move, he said to her, *don't dream,*
until I come back from the dead for you.

I will come back from the dead for you.

44.
The palace grounds flash steep and white in sudden lightning: the plan of one endless disaster. She lies in his deathgarden, graveyard of discarded machines, soundlessly weeping, wondering, beseeching him:

why do you always find me where I'm not?

45.
She climbs back onto the moat. Earth begins turning / toward the meteor showers of midsummer. The day is warm and the fire inside Scarlet has melted away the ice-ache of abandonment for now, brought her blood back to boiling

rage. She turns to face the castle, bracing herself for a collision whose impact will surely be deadly.

The corridors anticipate her; they empty, allowing darkness to flood in.

46.
I am somewhat desperate to speak to you, she writes to him in a note, but doesn't know where to send it. She raises her fist to bang on the door, then lowers it. *I don't know what I'm doing here,* she says aloud. The wide, drooping brown eye of a wilted sunflower regards her

joylessly.

47.
Language lives in alteration: here she is. Take two-measure words and press them together like lips to a wound. Love too much, love at all. He has two statues, Heaven and Hell; they are carved from identical jewels into identical forms.

*

He chews on a butterfly's ragged skin, watches the fish (curious): rippling emeralds with streaks of scarlet swimming lazily around. He snatches one up from the pond—his hands have always been quick—and places it on the cobblestone path that meanders through the massive garden adjacent to the deviltrees. He watches it drown in the abundance of oxygen. He keeps chewing.

48.
From the prince's own calligraphy we have on scrolls his thoughts
on pornography   and what makes a woman
a woman.

*

She listens to ancient trees stream upward to the cyanotic sky; the bloodriver to the east goes plundering past. She moves into a space wrought more by silence than song. He told her once that he sees external wounds as internal healing. Impossible with him to be innocent.

49.
The Queen feeds her son the poison Hatred, calls it Wisdom. *the wisdom to know what, Mother?* he asks her sleepily. *the wisdom to know the difference,* she replies. In her voice a pause hovers, wicked.

the difference between what, Mother? He peers at her through the slits of his mostly-closed eyes. For a moment, she wears the face of Atropos. *the wisdom to know when to shut up and eat your butterflies.*

50.
Nights like these, the edges blur into eternity, into a single red scream that begins with the heart's first beat and continues after the last breath expires, leaving the body

with only the fact of itself: a discarded skin-sac, rotting meat.

*

he sleeps and she sleeps; they dream the same dream:

(don't move.)
(don't dream.)
(don't even breathe

until I come back from the dead for you.)
But to live in his palace?
(I will come back from the dead for you.)

51.
Scarlet scatters instances
of herself like breadcrumbs; she spreads
the scent of her pale
-petal skin, disperses ample strands of her

momentarily platinum hair, and sets asunder
plethoric sections of each of her poems.
You can see desire go traveling into the dark
country of another soul: a place where cliffs break
off. Cold light like moonlight falling
on it. Soon her disseminated mementos
will strew themselves over the palace
grounds, perimeter
to perimeter.

52.
He sits on a bench in the park where the addicts score, her poetry wadded in his fists. No one has any reason to know who he is, but they do. Everyone who passes him has, in their eyes, a look of recognition (they bow their heads to hide it). He looks angry, *feels* vicious. He scowls, stuffs his plentiful jewels into his ample pockets.

*

Under his trembling eyelids, he tries to access his memories of her small, trusting face, her sweet, tentative smile, sunlit when it surfaced for him.

So many skin-scented memories; too many tearstained images of shattered sapphire eyes, their lemon streaks lit up like lightning. He licks her paper / words, addicted to the static crackling that offers up her essence (her permission notwithstanding).

53.
maybe I'll stay clean today, he mutters, post-stutter, stumble-drunk-and-high all last night— just like every other night. He fails, of course, but that's fine: he takes it one day at a time.

High again. *I'd rather be dead*
he says, *than sober.*

*

Heroin is the whore

he brings to their bed regardless of whether he lets Scarlet sleep beside him—or outside, in her car.

54.
For years—feeling lost, or overwrought and rotten—Scarlet stood outside his room, face pressed against the cold palace windowpanes, silently pleading with the prince / in him: *oh please, just once, speak my name.* He calls her *The Bitch* to his friends. Or *She*.

why won't you say my name! (Weeping now.) The lacerated sky leaking cobalt.

tell me my name! she screams. The queen casts Scarlet's reflection out of every mirror. The glass doesn't break: Scarlet does. The princeling giggles. The queen cackles. Even the dead king laughs, the terrible sound of emptiness colliding with itself.

55.
Shaking

herself free of so many killing memories, Scarlet discovers she is lost. After a 6½ hour trek, her legs are tired and weak; she finds herself / dispersed

as countless shatterpieces. What makes life life, and not a simple story? Jagged bits, never still, moving all along the soul.

56.
There is a third eye tattooed on the back of his neck, filled with winter, the better to watch her with. *I am writing,* she scratches on the paper, *that it is 5:04 a.m. my arms are hungry; my mouth is empty. inside me, there are spiders skittering around the hollow place where my mind should be.*

57.
Piano chords claw at the silence. Fermata of anguish, her keening
grief. (She never did learn how to play.)

58.
smash the plate glass window, he told her once. Road reverse, reverse road, take her home, take her home, take her
|cut|

59.
she's probably still on her damned laptop, hauling it around the parking lot, sitting with it between her slut legs, the queen's security chief tells Richard Tracey, the head of the palace's FBI task force.

*

The FBI papers the palace with warnings: *a great menace,* the signs say. *do not trust this girl slut.*

*

listen to the wind. the wind will tell you.

(The wind, the wind. Incessant
between her fingers.)

60.
He covers the scent of her with his hands, wiping more of her away with every furious swipe. He practices knifing the sunset with his original sin, the shade and shadows borne of it

and turns away: the snow sloshing off the tops of towers, all different heights and depths, has captured his attention.

61.
She cuts her hands on his diamonds.
He cuts his diamonds on her hands.

62.
She writes, *I will come back from the dead*
then crosses it out.

63.
He drives around in a BMW all day, which he cannot afford, looking to score.

64.
On the back of the bus, she composes parables that are very clever at imitation, very clever at imitation. They all tell her favorite story: through the narrowing hole of yesterday comes today. Through the widening hole of today comes the future, its massive burn

of light.

65.
Hot silver fog sweeps over the palace. The prince lies shrouded in sleep. From here, she can see the river filling its reed banks under the rapidly whitening sky. River life meditates on its surface: green silver black, tinctured with gold. The castle is still

in shadow: the severe marble arches and towering sentinel trees advise her not to enter: to run, run from the open mouth of these countless frayed and fleshless moments.

66.
All day long she has tried to cut out her tongue. If she could strain her thoughts clear of impulse, would her screams subside to mere desperation and lust? She's been here too long. Her syntax slips; her shadow wrenches itself from her feet, and slips free.

67.
Even the sky has grown stale: wet away-ness, desolation. The wind winds around the rain, an arrangement which shapes the peripheral shadows hanging

in the leaf-wrought sky.

68.
The queen fears biblical floods. It's a sensible fear: every full moon, the tides wash over the palace, and drown the jeweled fish.

69.
Waiting out the tidal floods, Scarlet examines the view from that last Thursday: what did it mean when the prince kissed her on the forehead (three times gently) before he stole her credit cards? (The cash she had, she'd handed over willingly.)

*

it's him every time, she types. *the prince in my stomach, the prince in my throat, my heart in his teeth.*

70.
A boy and a girl are one.
A boy and a girl and a royal blackbird are one.

71.
Scarlet presses on, past the landmark that has the audacity to still call itself

home.

72.
She holds a tiny, tear-shaped object in her hand: it resembles onyx in color, weight, and sheen. She closes her fingers over her palm, gripping it protectively, then swallows the sacred seed, this secret hope

-gift sent by a friend (presumed dead).

*

The seed reaches her stomach and speaks
its prophesy: *He will be the death of you, Princess.*
And you will be the death of yourself, too.

73.
Nothing left but mirrors in her former room, dust-covered and reeking of the past

tense. Her hands close into fists. Frantic, random, she runs out to the meadow. She did not invent this (so much as invite it in).

74.
Years before, the queen secretly doctored the palace blueprints; since then, further damage has befallen. Nobody wishes to inform her of this.

*

Everyone's close-lipped approach to Scarlet's arson surprises her. Even the queen, who would normally be screaming the requisite *off with her head!* just sits on her throne: only the shadow of a frown alters her sharp-featured face.

75.
Sometimes, bending in the intensity of the blazing light, Scarlet stops to pick crimson

flowers. She doesn't yet understand the difference between *dying* and *death*; she plunders the cemetery for poetry. She cannot tell the living from the dead: everyone looks like a corpse.

76.
Like Scarlet, Her Royal Highness is very clever, very clever at imitation. If the prince's particles merge with the girl's, then off with her head, of course. The queen is also gifted at the decapitation business (Scarlet notes).

*

Night again. Camping is hard
on the vertebrae. The prince used to love
to drive around. When they'd stumble across an accident
of beauty, he'd shout, *somebody remember this!*

She was somebody.
She always remembered it.

77.
The sun rises bloody again. Scarlet looks to the sour light that slopes down in broken-up slats from the mountain peaks. She thinks,
this is not what I wanted,
not what I intended,
not what I willed myself to be.

78.
In his heat, moments before her final burn, the prince raised her up to the moon, heavily suspended in the star-scarred sky. *be still*, she ordered herself. *breathe.* Midnight, he was deeply immersed in heroin's heavy-blanketed sleep, dreaming of her. She too dreamed. Her nightmares were thick, distorted, filled with his barbed partings.

79.
Scarlet stares down at her fingers, realizes she doesn't know what to write. She becomes a bit hysterical. She is possessed of certain practical knowledge, such as *stop writing when you don't know what to write*. But she doesn't. She waits for another damned idea to drench the pages.

80.
When the lights go out for the fourth time, she begins. *tonight*, she writes, *I will tell you what I have done that you wouldn't have.*

81.
She picks flowers |cut| She picks selves |cut| She picks mourning |cut|cut|cut|

82.
The snake hisses her death at her: another familiar, poisoned moment to determine where these new bodyscars will form. As Scarlet returns to the palace, she prepares for her beheading. Meanwhile, the prince has gone back to eating jeweled fish and butterflies.

*

When the lights go out for the final time, obscenity outsmiles silence. The night is thick with vermin crawling over garbage / heaps of composted heads, clocks spitting out split time.

83.
[Remnants of darkness. Scarlet arrives at the palace.]

Morning climbs cloud-vines into the sky. The girl knocks at the palace door; the queen greets her with a smile.

84.
I am ready for my beheading, the girl says. Timing is important. Exactitude is important. It's true that most natural facts elude her. *traitor!* screams the queen. She has no feet, but always wears long dresses to conceal it. A choir of dead, footless relatives surround her at all times so as not to betray Her Highness's perceived deformity.

85.
In order to repossess her soul, Scarlet believes, she must welcome this / beheading.

86.
She looks across the clearing. The answer is easy, she knows. Round, almost. Her head must be donated to science to further the study of love. She falls to the beaten earth.

87.
As she looks toward the words she's written, the queen closes the door and smiles. *I knew you'd be back.*

Of course you did, Scarlet says, neck titled.

88.
And someone else writes, *the end.*

89.
But it's not the end. It's easy to believe this alternative, easy to believe Scarlet will keep her head and reacquire the prince's love.

There is no place for her to say her prayers. No temple. No circle of holy stones.

90.
She thought she would get a goodbye kiss. O, this is a wicked ending, even for her sourblack life.

91.
The prince peers from behind the scrim. He puts his head to the wall, bites his tongue until he tastes blood. He kisses the stone, pretends it's Scarlet.

92.
(But the kiss tastes like dust.)

93.
don't move, she mouths to him,
don't dream,
don't even breathe
until I come back from the dead for you.
I will come back from the dead for you.

94.
don't worry, you will remain in my arms, he whispers to her. I will save your bones. I built you by water, and back by water you shall go. I will cast your ashes by the lake in the woods.

95.
off with her head! cackles the queen.

96.
this may require some dismantling, Scarlet thinks.

97.
The axe whistles down; her head is gone. Her eyelids blink once, watching her body twitch.

98.
The long sigh the deep sigh the red sigh that leaves her mouth is the final breath he takes before

99.
he writes his suicide note:
*don't move, don't dream, don't even breathe
until I come back from the dead for you.
I will come back from you.*

100.
And *did you exist ever did you* and pulls out the gun.

Mar 2012-Sept 2014

Part II: Except for Then

*I sit
Composed in...psyche-knot,
Rooted to your black look, the play turned tragic:
...such blight wrought...*

Sylvia Plath
"Conversation Among the Ruins."
The Collected Poems.

No Alembic

Every morning, I trek deep into deserts, where time's illimitable epochs permit visions of jeweled flowerpetals to fall, uninhibited, over the searing, variegated shades of sunlight on sand. I dream of ice-wings and scorchings, but waking provides no alembic; it permits no distillation of clarity. The stinging winds intensify, blurring the words of the pivotal question: when I was there, within reach—when I was thrashing on your palace steps, burnt by the blue flames of our dying star—*where were you?* I always find myself / caught at the bottoms of things, snared by the spaces in between, where every abyss asserts itself so that it might invade and rearrange the steady presence of the deep, uninterrupted light. I can hear the midnight screams of plummeting stars. The liquid-morphing shapes flickering on the ceiling descend to brand me with their seething colors.

Dispersal of breath, disposal of self, the moment that divides itself into countless / thousands of voids

Jan-Feb 2006
May 2011
Sept 2014

Michelle Greenblatt

Periphery and Precipice

These days I spend hours kneeling in front of the stone you gave me…But if the one is too much (as insanity constantly informs

me) then that which I desire so fiercely—to investigate violence, to seek life, and to find a goddamned answer

to what surrounds me—because if I don't, I'll be incapable

of understanding my surroundings: see, I only ever find suffering and its endless senselessness. The light we lost

so long ago is already transmuting itself from fact to memory. So despair drives me to the periphery, past the limit and over the precipice

of too-far-gone, where I can see

how fast and how far I've fallen. Having bypassed the cutting edge, I'll stand barefoot on the bleeding one, and I'll sway, brainless

as a blade of grass in the wind, waiting to decide when to jump. Because we are who we are, I can only be who I am, though Lord knows I've tried

to be otherwise.

"Just be happy if the warmth inside stays the warmth inside," Shannon tried to tell us, as recently as the week before she died. One of us should have known we couldn't survive alone. One of us should have warned

the other.

Oct 2005-Feb 2006
Jan-Oct 2010
Apr-Aug 2012
Feb-Sept 2014

Michelle Greenblatt

Catherine's Absence

Please post flyers, disseminate   information, never stop   asking / questions.
                    Pray, give her some of your time,
          because she gave all   of her blood.

To be selfish   was easy.   To be cruel.   To ignore Catherine,   to mock her   to cross
          her out was far
     too easy   for too many   people.

I think we all imagined   her mother's agony: try losing
          a child   to the fluctuating moods   of a monster
who wears your brother's   face,   try to imagine crawling

               into the dank   aphotic space
where Catherine's body remains,   to imagine your daughter dying; to have no hope
                    of ever   finding her.

and Catherine?   To be spellbound   by one's tormentors, to be desperate   for
                    acceptance, to be heartsick   for love
          was what Catherine lived   (and died)   through   each day.

With no hope   of being   found, Catherine could only   wonder
     if she would be remembered.   I know that's what she thought of
                    in the end.

It made dying
          that much harder.

ASHES AND SEEDS

Jan-Feb 2006
Jan-Oct 2010
Apr 2012

Michelle Greenblatt

Atomic Time

        dear Aidan,

at the hospital, an elderly man
with a concerned voice
the color of dull metal-grey catching
on plain, scratchy beige. His kind
blue eyes, the color of faded denim, offered me
empathy as his thin, age-lined lips asked
my name. he didn't ask me, *who* did *this*
        to you?
instead he asked,
                what does the color red feel
                like when it's hurting you
                          on the inside?
                and *is there anything I can do*
                to make it stop?

bruises and bite-
marks crisscrossed
my breasts.

I remember
the letter on that kindly man's hat, that blood
red "m" like the first letter
of my name, crimson
and crumbling, steaming scarlet
rivulets of *aa* lava, spiny and jagged, which will split a person's
skin, easy

as slitting / fish. you always laughed
when I said that
letters have colors, noises have textures,
tastes have shapes and sounds. The letter
"c", particularly when capitalized, smells
delicately fragrant: it captures the silken, frangible yellow
of wind
-caressed petals, their delicate
scent released.

You told me I was crazy when I explained that
a lower
case "i" always feels like the sloppy, slippery insides
of a cucumber. "i" is something dirty, a coming
apart—something breaking
down. "i" makes
my fingers filthy—filthy as that night you left me
                        trapped with the man
                        holding the gun
                        to the soft underside of my chin
                        in the back of that dingy alley.

then came his sourblack acts.

as I obeyed, I could feel the metal
tip of his gun warming
against my skin.

when I cried, it took little chinks out of me. I shed
layers of my former self while he watched
and laughed, laughed at me. I stood

on my small red-Michelle
shadow, hurting her, but I stood there, waiting
for the skin to grow
back, for the holes
to sew themselves
closed.

*

at the hospital, it was blankwhite. not the walls,
which were also blankwhite, but rather, being there.
being there *hurt*. There I was, the blank slate upon
which the poetry
of erasure
        was being written.

no one asked about my ripped.
no one said, "why are there bite-marks
on your breasts?" they only asked, "what color
is a hospital?" and "are you the color of death?" or was that
me, asking myself, rocking in the cold waiting
room, making noises like a wounded
animal. The cold was a noose
of ice around my neck.

I kept looking at my wristwatch, and at the clocks
on the walls. they were all horribly wrong;

I could only think, the cesium
133 isotope is the one most commonly used
to make atomic clocks. the number 133 is a frost-white ice-blue ice-blue ,

which makes it the color of roses
on sheet cakes, makes it the color of winter, but very
volatile.

*

when I came out of the hospital, my anger was total.
there were no colors, no letters,
no poems, no words. I was still young enough
to taste my death
in my mouth.

Dec 2005
Jan-Oct 2010
Apr-Oct 2011
Apr 2012

Michelle Greenblatt

Songs of Elemental Change

I snatch stray prayers on their ascent to Heaven, hoping to rise with them, making every attempt to penetrate its locked gates. Once again turned away, I kick over bits of interstellar dust, dislodging cinderblocks from the moldering walls of the tumbledown tenements. Heartsores and eyesongs, binary code of the heart, each festering. How shall I greet thee, Winter, after you have wrought such destruction? All songs of elemental change are forever silent now. I am the embodiment of what you've done to me—Aidan, this is what you've done to me—my eyes are dead moons:

they no longer reflect any light.

Dec 2005
Jan 2010
Apr 2011-Apr 2012
Feb 2014

Half-life.

This is our half-life: we are carbon, we drink fire, we continue to degrade... Trapped in glass, you tell me it's over—but it's never really over. This is the way our "love" "dies": suffering the erratic rhythms of our faulty hearts. Each of the usual signs is a psychotropic microcosm of the world we lived and loved in, has an echo, and knows nothing

that would be of use to us. How do the dead summon us? With prayers. Destruction sleeps, dreaming fitfully inside a hungry volcano. At night, I dream of you. You cover me with Lorca's dead kisses. You are the narcosis I crave during the abandonment of each day. You hide

the sacred / scriptures of sleep, which each night's sculpted moon once held in its hands (empty now). Grief seals us in our bodies like stopgap and anthologizes emotion as we scrape backwards, always backwards, our bodies banging against the shore. I am a long line painted in the urgencies of sand

-drawings as they are wiped away by the soaking hand of the sea: I do this because this is what you've done to me. I set our story down as the days pile high as trash heaps...I didn't learn what I never asked and I never asked what I needed to learn. I guess this is what it's like to fly over you.

Dec 2005
Apr 2011
Apr 2012-Aug 2012
Feb-Sept 2014

Michelle Greenblatt

Yours Now

In the dark, there is only the sound of you. Whether dead or alive, you are never mine. I see you in the drugstore pharmacies. Your body braced against the plaster walls, you beg, spreading your hands in supplication. Pale-faced, you turn to me and scream, *We are fragments!*

Fragmenting along, I whisper as I turn away. I will repeat what you told me that night the darkness seemed to extend itself forever. If one changes the usual order of awakenings and recites altered versions of the oldest omens and prayers, the most ancient of all gods will appear.

I can no longer remember the names of flowers we once collected and treasured. Your body is newly tattooed; this remind me you are no longer mine. The abyss you created to sew inside me has taught me that fate takes pleasure / in its punishments. It prefers its food alive

and fighting. You confiscated my possessions; you call them yours now—why? I have lain awake among the sexual flowers since the beginning, clutching the relics of our youth tightly to me. And I have longed for you.

Dec 2005
Apr 2011-Apr 2012
Feb-Sept 2014

The Names of the Dead

The doors only speak in sullen, occasional syllables; the windows have no words at all. I stand on the steps of the madhouse, stretching my arms out to the stars. This restlessness is what causes these vessels to constrict, dangerously weakening every cell

wall inside me. You've dropped me down your starscorched quarry: strewn with the dim-lit wreckage—the scattered shatterpieces of celestial bodies. This is where you remake me, time / after time. I must appear lifeless

as a mannequin: you amputated my arms and severed my legs; my porcelain-made breasts are smooth, nippleless now. I retrace my steps, tiptoeing down the meridian dividing the cold

streets of this anonymous city where the wind sweeps down from the tenements' black, collapsing structures. Beneath the gold coins, these maddened cork-screw eyes of mine are clouded by Hades' dust

again. Your shadow touches mine, reminding me of life's dangling edges, its tender penetralia. I won't sleep tonight, remembering you. My head is a zoo of caged letters and malformed words spelling out the sparks

of sentences that cool to ash before I am able to utter them. Who will whisper these thoughts into the lowercased heavens when you have left me lost / in the waiting

fog which remains hidden amid the damp, gutted boulevards? A murder of crows caterwauls across the weak-sunned winter sky, streaking it black with their extended, unruly feathers. I still lose

Michelle Greenblatt

my balance when you resurrect my dreams. *You're not enough,* you say to me, *for this to ever be.* Asleep beneath the twisted, lifeless limbs of a leafless deviltree, a thin shroud of starlight burns

its way out through the cloudcovered sky. The dead rub their black hands against my face, claiming me, and still you won't permit me to speak

your name. I'm just one more body you've had / to bury and unbury over the past decade. Who alone remembers the names of the dead? No cemeteries, no crosses, no graves. I do. I do.

Jan 2006
Apr 2011-Apr 2012
Feb-Sept 2014

Terrible Fires

Everything goes all of a sudden white—then blazes ochre, crimson and sulfur. Lightning strikes / terrible fires. You grab fistfuls of my hair and rip them out by bleeding roots, leaving torn sections of ravaged scalp behind. You snatch my screams as they

burst out of me; you store them in the same glass bottles where you trap my dreams. The thick core of your carefully-constructed silence presses against my bulletproof

windows from the inside / out. As the moon rolls its luminous bulk across the black-blanketed sky, you ask me about the lengthy metaphors I fashioned after you

dragged me (bound and gagged) through the cloud-covered distances last year. I have no answers for you: I can't stop singing. I never stop shaking. When I rest, it's only for seconds

at a time. Your features streak as you take your paintbrush to our globe and smack the North grey and black—causing it to crack and buckle under me as you deliver your lecture of perverted pauses. And when you touch me, that part of my body freezes and then falls away.

Jan-Mar 2006
Apr 2011-Apr 2012
Feb-Sept 2014

Michelle Greenblatt

Call My Name, I'll Bring the Rain

We pour liquor down our throats, pretend it is love. I plow the seeds of all your alcoholic tomorrows, planting their sour grains alongside the great felled beast, time: Time will tell, the saying goes, but time no longer tells

us anything. The leaves winter knocked loose from the black locust trees circle down the eddying, bracken meltwater; its murky rivulets steal every reflection. Above us, the molten sun bakes the grey clouds into scorched-white sterility.

*

After you harvest the sun, call my name, I'll bring the rain. I'll give you my oxygen when the air turns to cinders: it won't hurt / as much to burn. *I know it hurts to burn.*

I'll still be fragile from frost; I'll have no exits to offer you. I will forever be caught in the bloodmirror you forged for me. I'll do what you want, what you need, whatever you ask of me; I'll be anything

you tell me to be. Call my name, I'll bring the rain. I'll dangle from the middle of a phrase. I'll dig my own grave. Just come back, come back to me.

May 2011
May 2012
Feb-Aug 2014

Shadows Turn Bright

The woodlands remember me. They catch my scent, and remember. I can still hear the evisceration of shadows

as the sun's scorch-light burns them

away. Now comes the life-pulse of the forest, the low throbbing of bees, the vibration of dew landing on quivering leaves, and the scumbled treeflowers humming

their pulsations, life-songs and affirmations which are still,

for the most part, ignored. The long, wind-beaten grassblades continue to camouflage snakes. I buried you in the tone-deaf garden, miles away from this

place. But it seems I spoke too much and too soon for you continue to lie

to me, even amid our sacred, secret circle of stones: you will not rise again even though the combustible treeline is freezing

and I'm begging you

to, even though the record keeps skipping and my skin is beginning to singe— never worry: I will stay 'til it's all burned away.

Jan 2006
May 2011-May 2012
Feb 2014

Michelle Greenblatt

I Am Blackness Walking

Out, damned spot!

>William Shakespeare
>*Macbeth*
>Act V, Scene i. *ll.* 2159

The constellated wind knocks at my heart. I am blackness walking

through the clotted white void. Lick my skin, you will taste burnt
paper; touch my heart, it will feel like tar. Bathed in mercurochrome, I imbibe

emptiness; when I am sated, the hissing whispers return

to remind me, *Aidan's destroyed / every emergency
exit; now you are trapped beneath the icy undersides of his carefully constructed*

oubliette...But forgive me, the house is a mess: he's thrown the corpses

of my former selves into every cobwebbed
corner and strewn his slashed canvases across the floor. I tried

to warn you: his way of painting always involved undressing me with his eyes.

May 2011
May 2012
Mar-Sept 2014

ASHES AND SEEDS

The (W)hole of the Unknown

> *The weapons*
> *that were once outside*
> *sharpening themselves on war*
> *are now indoors*
> *there, in the fortress.*
>
> > Margaret Atwood
> > "The Circle Game" part v.

Under salvo, I fall through the black
cataracted path of your perceptions; our past collapses in
an avalanche of ash, the downrush
of memories exploding
like artillery fire.

These days, I need copious amounts
of supplemental oxygen just to breathe: you've strung
electrical wires through the pierced organs
of my failed poetry.

Today marks three years since you petrified
my kidneys. *In darkness, I handed you*
my heart. With my nails, I continue scratching
our story onto the face of your cave. In the void, two translucent
half-moons took shape, imprisoning me
between seven years of hermetically sealed
parentheses.

Michelle Greenblatt

In those epochs
of winter, your face hovered over me, an unmanned predator
drone cruising my mind's dark corridors, raining
down the chemicals that deranged my memory: eras
of Celan's black milk and poison-clotted honey.

Together we cultivate only
snakes. Twilight, the stars start
to flicker; distant echoes
of emptiness haunt the evening
languor before dissipating
into the (w)hole / of the unknown.

Hollow me out a grave I will come home.

Jan 2005
May 2011
May 2012
Mar-Sept 2014

Burning Leaves in Hollywood Hills Park

for Irene Shemony

The wind curves its arms 'round my hips, plucks my face to blushing with frigid fingertips, grips my hair at the roots and pulls 'til I bleed.

I think I even stumbled in the pure places, though they were few, and only occurred where the wind was indolent.

I remember you laughed at me for forgetting things like balance. The ground was as grey as the sky; the chillblue Atlantic licked me

with a frilled tongue until the (w)hole of me turned to bloodless filaments. *Master has a mistress*, Ocean whispered; *Mistress is master*. There was a pause, a sustained sense

of ugliness. How can I fight this? was the logical question. I think I was still trying to believe that nothing would go wrong. I was 14. Irene and I were burning

leaves in Hollywood Hills Park. Even then, I was dreaming of darker fires.

Jan-Mar 2006
May 2011
May 2012
Mar-Aug 2014

Michelle Greenblatt

From the Shadowside

I crawl over the bleak-beige, treeless plains on scraped knees, my hands bleeding. The land barely varies cadence; it casts no victims down

before me. Panting, sunburnt plants affix me with their pistil-and-stamen glare—all trampled flowers and withered, trembling leaves—and bend under the blacksyrup

sky, awash with the stars' brilliant indifference: the prerogative of all ancient things. Whisper of wind against the small, polished surfaces

of glass: I see your ghost in every reflection, a gash of emerald firelight embedded in each eye. Long threads of essence

-red hang from cirrocumulus clouds. I press my face to the scalding mirror-lacquered sand, listening for a hoof

-beat, a heartbeat, a way to beckon me back home—and from the shadowside, answers arrive: *with your echoes, your emptiness, and your terrible absence of light.*

Jan 2005
May 2011
May 2012
Mar-Aug 2014

A Silver Sliver of Moon

A silver sliver of moon shivers and breaks away, plummeting through the frigid wind into the expectant limbs of a yew tree. The black vault you hide me in at night offers up casks of emptiness and jugs of sour wine. I pour out the contents according to ritual, imbibe them with proper ceremony. Years ago, I learned to take nourishment from nothingness. Long will I dwell here, longer will I draw upon this unexpected source of strength. And when I rise, I shall rid you of your painted sunsets, your watercolored skies; I'll give you back this blackened canopy of ash, and return your vile wine. I will free myself from your bed of roseless thorns. I will rise from this cenotaph.

I was on fire and you didn't care. Kyle did.

Feb 2006
May 2011
May 2012
Mar-Sept 2014

Michelle Greenblatt

Nicotine and Time

Life is a burning up of questions.

> Artaud
> "Here Where Others..."

I sit before the flickering fire, hypnotized by the wrath of flames. Nicotine and time have stained my fingertips. At the knife-edge

of insomniac consciousness, the febrile quiescence of the night trembles. Embroidering the surrounding hills, the rising

fog cloaks me, voiding me with malicious glee. The aspen trees sway as they scrape against the rice-paper horizon. You took your knife

to me. Because you were bored; because you could. It made you feel powerful. My poetry is little

more than scrap paper now. The stars boil; caterwauling across the Crayola-black blanket of sky, they devour

themselves. Meanwhile, I try to forget myself in the tedium of endurance: the ceaseless rainfall, the many medicated

occasions, the rest of my life / without you. It is difficult to hear and all but impossible to see when you've halved my heart-notes and burned my poetry. Still, I embark down the thorn-and-thistle nightmare whose path you mapped out

for me. At first I am overly cautious. I consider friendship / a waste. I stumble back to the winter orchard, where black branches thicken under crumbling

arches of variegated sky. You are painting my portrait: my cirrocumulus smile will obtain a single moment

of splendor; until then, you add the essentials: a crown of barbed wire, two bracelets of razors, a necklace of coal. You jackknife the dead

meadow until the bloody spokes of sunlight fissure the fields with deadly fires; you bind my love to the ghostly lure

of rheumy corners. Even now, I hear the black rustle of wings: it is death, finally come for me.

Feb-Mar 2006
May 2011
May 2012
Mar-Sept 2014

Michelle Greenblatt

No Metronome

Panic, that old familiar
torment, is back: blackbile
-terror nails her
to the wall. Standing in a corner she keeps
dustless as possible, and free
of roaches, she brings
back her battle

-scarred lexicons
and dons her anticipatory
armor, built to withstand the cloud
-bombed gales that precede his deadly
damage-games.

*

Wisps
of lacy moonlight keep the clock
performing / its tick tock
torture. She asks no
questions of time

as it passes: she can't trust her senses: she believes
no metronome.

*

In the harsh tidal night, the stars continue
to fall, galactic
glass

shattering against the sharpened obsidian
spikes / of midnight.

She stands on a dark
minute, tick-tock, tick-tock. All she can hear
are the seconds scraping toward the past
tense.

Feb 2005
Mar-May 2011
May 2012
Apr-Sept 2014

Michelle Greenblatt

Salt

Lamination across the shivering
sky where a thick, constant drizzle
of chemicals passes for perpetual
rain; the atmosphere's wet
melodies claw
through stagnant bog
-silence. The ruminant corpse lashed
to night's cunning
wings threads the current
song with its long silver
needles. The temporal closes
over the sensate; oceans evaporate, leaving
only salt, only salt. The pace of light falters,
slower now than the speed
of sound.

Feb-Mar 2006
May 2011
Apr-Sept 2014

My Light with Your Teeth

We return to the field where, under the buttersun, we once made love in the lush springtime grass. Tonight, standing on the singed pastureland, the sky snarls keloids of stars in my hair. Wielding your scissors between my thighs, you pull at my light with your teeth. I am edged with you struck me last. Now comes the frost, now comes the flood. The preening, cumulous pose you struck after you tossed me in that garbage can nine years ago was enough to make my summer muscles go dark, marbleized.

Feb-Mar 2006
May 2011
May-Sept 2014

Michelle Greenblatt

Operatic Blurrings

I breathe between operatic blurrings each day; I bleed between the ocular dualism that strikes every night. I'm half / child this morning, though it's *not* morning. I've learned I'm extinct

enough theoretically to pass for it in actuality. You strew heaps of memories onto the piles of dirty laundry in your bedroom, forcing the air into feeling dirty—an old trick you used

to play on me when I was called *fiancée*—now I am forced to focus on all the mail that's beached itself on my desk. I try to call you but you've changed your number

and the telephone has morphed into a miasmic taunt. I lay my head against the ground and pretend it is sky.

Mar 2006
May-Sept 2014

About Tenses

Nightclouds crisscross the sky at the apex of stars and darkness. No use dancing tonight; the beams of the searchlights are still out, staining the sky. Time froths forth as you laugh too much and talk too often about tenses, refusing to meet my eye.

Mar 2006
Sept 2014

How We Died, All Those Times

1. Shadow Hand-Holding

Stiff-jointed, I stretch to write tonight instead of chasing your vague ecstasies: circle after circle, I have written to you and for you, but will it ever be enough? The display of sharp teeth in the jagged smile cutting across your face, in the crepuscular light I know the answer:

Not now. Not ever. The river-rhymes escape, splattering against the grass. We stand in the doorway of our broken home. The pigments of your surprise dance around your head in flaring-red tinctures. The first sign of change was when your shadow's hand let go of mine.

2. Widening

It's evening. Brodsky's sun sets on an empty horizon. The cool air animates my frame, but inside I'm sluggish. I sit and drum my finger on the cobblestones. Sorry for the intrusion: it's just my loneliness again, widening. *From now on and evermore,* one of us vows, and the other nods, not hearing. We peel the dead bark off the devilwood trees.

3. Neither of Us

We built a home out of scrap-heap stone. Emptiness, that thing that swallows sunlight, is an amalgam of rejectamenta: mottled mirrors and miasmic dreams. We take our deaths in small doses. I place my lips on yours. Neither of us moves. Neither of us breathes.

Mar 2006
Sept 2014

Michelle Greenblatt

The Name I Once Went By

The name I once went by is tattooed under my tongue. The greenery that grows around me goes bold, then dark. The incisions slashed across my cheeks widen when I speak.

I try always to give him the truth, but the facts slip through my language, a system of mutually enacted paradoxes: outside and inside, space and surface, love and lust. Be careful:

they reverse. A single random growth of morning promises to pare away the layered silence. Winter dies, her throat slit, though the wind is still cold against my face, my arms, my breasts.

He is blind like history; he makes me uninstall the grand, unfurling instances of penetrating remembrance. His hands burrow into the soil and come up worms.

I am kept alive in this house where shadows burn when the light strikes; reason chainsmokes the answers, throwing ashes this way, seeds that way.

Mar 2006
Sept 2014

Beginning with Distance

Possessed by dreams of him, I move through nighttime's bleak ascension. In the kaleidoscopic brilliance of my nightmares, he is as chill as the wind. Black wings flee the scene, chipping

the varnish off the sky. The scene cracks open: here I am, outside at 4:09 a.m. I don't mind the quiet, the way it so brashly contradicts my heavy breathing. The thick gauze of darkness wrapped around my face swallows virgin sounds.

After the fear and the fight / depart, I hold my wounds together with my hands. Every dream I have is a conjecture of the culminations that begin with distance. And every night, little bits of veneer break away from my mind. When I said I felt lonely, he asked me to describe it.

Mar 2006
Sept 2014

Pound and Flutter

Nocturnal gardens lush with nightfruit and iridescent flowers creep up the walkway, calling me to them, nectar-sweet. The ground bleeds like cut gums. This place festers with you. Between the rows wrought with glistering permutations, along each

poisoned edge: me. This garden is metric (by which I mean, *Come closer, I can't hear you.*) I will forfeit the scene, I will summon the dead: I'll do whatever you want me to. The abstract-theoretical states that you are (the consciousness) here, the figurative and literal.

The garden's breath draws earth / and sky closer. Its portals smell of saffron; its flowers' arrested light meets secreted sound. And those black wings: how I ache to grab them, to feel their pound and flutter crush between my two small hands.

Some name you once went by circles the dawn bearing down on the garden of nightfruit and iridescent flowers. When I mention you, the dark snake hisses *Duplicate* to Her Majesty. On nights like tonight, you will tell me another story of lies.

Mar 2006
Sept 2014

Hypothermic Silence

We weigh our grief by the gram then sell it accordingly. I paint the combustible horizon as the hypothermic silence closes in around me. The stems of flowers twitch; the sun erupts, sending flaming streaks of scarlet, scorched orange, and burnt yellow ribboning across the sky. This is a place where sighs stay trapped in ice. Suddenly I'm running. Some universal cataclysm hangs over this valley of the dead…Here, see my poetry? Four and a half years ago, I traveled hundreds of miles to bring it to you; you shot me upon sight. The hole in my head continues to brazenly widen. I keep my smile pinned in a locket 'round my neck so it will never abandon me again. I am pinned, tender-red, against the smoking sky.

Mar 2006
Dec 2013-Sept 2014

Michelle Greenblatt

Committment above All

Light clatters blindly downward; I stand in a dark valley, weary of my form. The windowsills don't answer questions when I open my eyes to ask; the rats screech something like a song. You breathe onto the solitary snow, crack starlight Her Majesty surrounds by barbed wire. *Stay*, commands the Queen, who looks for commitment above all. She casts her shadow by the doorway. The king winces, underfoot, while she supplants a village with rotten sacking. Her head is full of antifreeze; she uses an electric blanket for comfort.

Silent, everything is silent / after the flood of cinders turns to a floor of tiny windows.

Mar 2006
Sept 2014

Corpus Delicti

You button the nothing closed with deft fingers. March is when I start to remember you, when the greenery sets fire to my mind. You are the unknown photographer who sits, snapping pictures of the grey.

*

One theory: you are carbon / dust recovering latent fingerprints. All I think about are endings. You bind me with light, pierce me with sound. A clump of cirrocumulous clouds seals my mouth.

*

Under the flexing orange sky the sun shines black and cold. From the peak of the city, the wolf lopes softly down, licking her lips in salty concentration. This plethora of paint is your cover-up for skin.

*

Following years of scarcity, you finally bare your form. The scissor-wind snip-snips my hair, cut / up to my neck on the battlefront of my body. Like any life, you never return. The ambulance siren silent.

Mar 2006
Sept 2014

Michelle Greenblatt

The Cartographer's Diagnostics

I travel along the map's edge according to your diagnostics, but to your dismay. I'm restless as the ocean before a hurricane, and silent as the birds. No crying anymore. I'll stop trying to deceive myself: I don't love this mutilated world. I know only one thing: scarcity rules landscapes like these.

After several days of struggle, I cultivate my suffering into words (but do not speak them). I'm steady, steady as the drumming summer sun. I try to confess to you, the long silver rod I stole has conducted no lightning since stolen. Fulminated against the flowers, I watch the Queen eat her children.

Life is transformed into still / life. Dark foliage brushes your cheek. When you're finally asleep, I have time to notice the long winter and kiss your impatient mouth, which speaks a language I'd forgotten for years. My identifying features uncover decomposition between each kiss.

I am up all night, and exhausted every day. I am afraid to look at you: your dilated eyes are sacs of undelivered promises; you would not recognize your destination if slapped in the face with a seismic tremor. I writhe in the dark, body battered by sick blood. Lying next to you, my flesh is as dry as can be.

I carve out phrases for you that startle me. I cling to the letter that repeatedly reject my paper with deliberate steps and disturbing hygiene. Underpowered and overwhelmed, we paddle through the ultra-violet light. We peer into the lens of the eye; we bend the air backwards. Eventually we stop / searching for what we came for.

Mar-Apr 2006
Sept 2014

Snake in the Grass

Nightflowers bloom along the cliff. The nectar thickens. An adder slithers through the grass. The harvest moon. The rotted tulips. The unopened book. Are: images in her head she transcribes onto soiled paper. And then there is the kiss, the effort to pin her down with his lips. *You are a masterpiece*, he whispers in her ear. Beads of perspiration drip from his forehead; his teeth are like talons. She screams. The seawater rots. She jumps.

Mar 2006
Sept 2014

Michelle Greenblatt

Let There Be Thorns

I turn the door with a changeling key; it opens a window that morphs into polyphonic words. I wind a garland of asphodels around the knife

you plunged into my corpse. You catch angels with a butterfly net. I sit and embrace a sewer, wearing your arms as a belt. I praise the sea; it is a heartbomb

between us. Distance keeps its promise. I throw off my clothes in front of the glare of the fireplace, the blacker / violet flames, the colder moon, and I dream

of spoils. I sever the ceaseless linger-scent of our embrace, our promises painted on the walls. Two-tone dreams cause journeys to end

between here and fields of fire. Failing to actualize, I push myself away with slit handprints, leaving bloodsmears on the papers where I cut

and pasted long lines from previous poems. Yet there's still no alternative to this smallness. Look with the wind's eye. Judging from

the wide vision of my face's wounded windows, I walk as one familiar with the way into the woods. My body,

into the furrowed mountains; my skull, into the undergrowth. I've failed to articulate the fact that we who are dead didn't begin

this way, in such looted darkness. I hack away the plants that bear briars; I turn over every corpse to look for answers, but I've become irrelevant. Let there be thorns. You press through the darkness that encloses window-vision as the clouds whorl away from the trees

felled by your axe. Laughing, you applaud as they topple. You think I'm not humble? I'm damned / if I sing, damned if I don't. Down

in the muddy depths of the stream beside our yellowed town, next to the windowpane where my wan face presses its weight against the glass, you burn

flowers. Dusk clatters forth. I stumble into the tones of the stone-songs summoned by my lamentations. I listen for a while as dusk passes. Darkness fills me up.

Mar-Apr 2006
Sept 2014

Michelle Greenblatt

Novocain

The seed prevails as symbol when bare-handed tentacles scavenge the ground for mountain- waste and claim the last redundancy

passed on to insistent downpour. A deluge inert as a corpse's heartbeat and as uncompromising as a demand might insist the ancient

crackle at the back of my skull is sickness: pulsating in and out by deeper degrees—cortex candy best for ruminations on prosthetic

poses which reap rewards: nothing more than asymmetrical allusions to aged lovers. As poetry changes

to prose and alienator actuaries deliver a wealth of blank space, I realize I have missed this / Novocain.

Mar 2006
Sept 2014

Subject and Icon

We bring our blood to the Dead / Sea, where we slaughter the last of the mammoths. We teeter on the razor's edge where windows are just cutting

ledges. We both live alone on unapproachable islands. The soot dampens; the night thickens. You flick your forked tongue at me, collecting poison

behind your teeth. Your devoted Purist servants repeat your messages until they're certain I won't forget your lessons—but I've never forgotten a single

one of them. I don't learn by repetition; it's your forced quickening of my pulse that works its curses—and still, my isolation continues. Possible futures creep by on passive

limbs; even the water droplets echo memories of your latex / bribery, lurching forward with that certain truancy inherent to teenaged children. A ductile place

of bright, complex greys exists where someone will want to play, so I swim downstream toward the mesmerizing

architecture of your foundations. The constant progress of static sound releases little barbs of energy that scratch at

the machinations of the movement-makers, howling death into the living / places before releasing the helpless into the arterial lull of bloodsong. This delays the visiting royalty while forcing them toward the inevitable center of consciousness orbiting our native thoughtground: transitive hellish, landscapes (the penumbral

consequence of rumination). In the locust-drip silence, this summer is wind-honed and filled with the molten cries for the merging of subject

and icon. The granite-topped waves reveal their sinuous riptide vagaries as if we'd stumbled into an aquatic

center for living life backward. Sentient lines underpin the stone-circles where time first asserted itself, and form and space forbade the moon's phases.

Mar 2006
Sept 2014

Formerly Enchanted

In the chaos and confusion of his cluttered closet space, slipshod with detritus, he rummaged around for a brutal weapon to press against the pale

prone neck of young Scarlet. Now she—dutifully carrying the dusty old waterjugs to quench the tired

fires burning on the scorched earth of his encampment—is the only one who can rend the night with the deadly-sharp blade of his black

knife. Sheering down the steeper side of the mountain, they descend lower and lower through the ocean of emptied-out light. The mountain-peaks clamber past. As a man

formerly enchanted, he knows that at the sound of a turning key he will lock down every entry-point she carved onto his body

and sewed within his mind because women are liars; they never stop thinking. Not for a moment do they stop

plotting. Everywhere, he leaves dead things / for memories. He's nursing his plethoric collection of old wounds when she approaches

the isle of sacrificial women. The night further narrows her eyes. She climbs his hill of skulls and stands at the top, searching

for him against the broad, blood-rimmed horizon. There's an etching of a sun on the stones, half-hidden now

Michelle Greenblatt

by smoke. He is furious; she feels road-killed. She wanted to find one law to cover all of living: she found fear, instead. A map of her nightmares is the only way out of here.

Mar 2006
Feb-Sept 2014

Ante-Mortem

> *A miracle is all that's keeping me*
> *from killing you.*
>
> > A Perfect Circle
> > "Orestes"

In the abandoned subway below the drumming
of rain and regrets, I hide
from the haloed-black
portents hacked
from snatches of slithering
shadows, I whisper, *Tell me, please, about*
what I dreamed last

night. And then weep: I believed him, I believed
him when he said he'd kill me
with his .9 mm Smith & Wesson. You hold out

your arms, but there's no protection against his trick
deck of fate-cards. Each star. Every self
-sharpening weapon, my friend, hones its blades,
gouging watchful
eyes into the walls. He's in the wind, fashioning
grass-blades into garrotes. Inside the glass
bottle, my ship constricts.

Michelle Greenblatt

Here
is this (ravenous) poetry,

from my hand to his,
always.

Aug 2005
Dec 2013

Except for Then

A monster inhabits me: lacuna, caldera, womb, home. It crawls out of me with grasping claws, rasping nightmare songs. Turn away from the haloed, sodium glow of the city's streetlamps—its skyscraper windows flaring panes of bleached light—and the night is black. It was always been black, except for then, when you were mine, and flowers came / thrusting up through the small cracks in the grey, trodden cement. Then people began to come by—mostly to see if I was still alive—so I spilled my usual mess of lies / all over the worried faces of my friends asking their gentle questions. I thought of myself, of turning into you. There had been sunlight for a while, but you sent it away again.

Mar 2006
May 2012
Feb-Sept 2014

Part III: The Perpetual Principles of a Dream

and as we lie
here, caught
in the monotony of wandering
from room to room, shifting
the places of our defenses,

I want to break
these bones, your prisoning rhythms
(winter,
summer)
all the glass cases,

erase all maps...

I want the circle
broken.

Margart Atwood
"The Circle Game" part vii.

The cage-dance.

> *Why art thou yet so fair? shall I believe*
> *That unsubstantial death is amorous,*
> *And that the lean abhorred monster keeps*
> *Thee here in dark to be his paramour?*
>
> William Shakespeare
> *Romeo and Juliet*
> Act V, Scene iii. ll. 102-105

His pet playmate paces over the hard-paved grey stones of her 6' x 8' cell with increasing frequency, now that he's made her possessions less accessible. Now that he's made her possessions less accessible, his pet playmate screams almost constantly. Hour after changeless hour, he haunts her / dreams. The cycle begins afresh at sunset: his shadow-cloaked revenant chases her into the opaque shimmer of the ceaseless, steaming summer evenings and into the myriad, insomniac hours. He hunts her during afternoons bloated by sticky, wanton heat; he pursues her into the dirty-deep he embeds in every identical night. He yanks her to her feet, commands her to dance. His laughter ricochets off her cell walls. He knows everything—everything but what she dreams. She sharpens her smile. He spins her through the downward spiraling silence of the strophic, stratified nights; he twists her / arm as he drags her through the rancid winds blowing in from the black sloughs. These seven years caged, she's spent endless days learning precious lessons: how to disguise her teeth / filed to fangs, how to forge her own warmth. All of the hope he's certain he smote shields a small, protected flame. Alone, she begins to ravel / her secret walls of stored-up breaths. Having finally mastered an escape, they snake their way out of her stone cage to travel the coastal waves of the midnight sea.

Michelle Greenblatt

Fear as preliminary to inevitability; every photographer asks, *May I have this dance*; pray these words are merely coincidence

Mar-Apr 2006
May 2012
July 2013
Feb-Aug 2014

Exsanguination.

Over the summer, weeds thicken; they cling to my legs when I walk from my house to yours. I stroll past the buffer of water that borders the west end of our yards; I wear nothing / but the nude-colored dress you bought me on my 18th birthday. I carry within me a molten image of need. These ancient stones crack open in the malicious animal-heat. You despoil even my shallowest breaths, sculpting them into a prison of hypnosis to keep me / caged. Hunting me, you decreate all space; straining against your imposed stillness, we bleed out. For the life in me, I cannot look away.

Afterdusk shimmer, last brilliant glimmer, heaven tears open / into emptiness

Mar 2006
May 2012
July 2013
Feb-June 2014

Michelle Greenblatt

Against the grey.

> *And you play the safe game*
> *the orphan game*
>
> *the ragged game*
> *that says, I am alone*
>
> *(hungry: I know you want me*
> *to play it also)*
>
> > Margaret Atwood
> > "The Circle Game" part vi.

With subcyaneous eyes, she stares out the attic window into the last pale sliver of shivering sky. Her words peel off the page, ink rising into the singed air. Hands trembling, she struggles to light the final match: one last chance to fend off the approaching void. She rips at the shadows; the shadows rip back. Once the candle is lit, its paltry light stretches and breaks against the grey, revealing the fissures in the ceiling as they open into emptiness.

Extended pauses, stammering transformations, no breathing in this / endlessness

Mar-Apr 2006
May 2012
June 2013
Feb-June 2014

Almost liquid.

> *For I myself have many tears to wash*
> *Hereafter time, for time past wronged by thee.*
>
> > William Shakespeare
> > *Richard III*
> > Act IV, Scene iv. ll. 299-380

To explore the nature of dis/trust. To scrub stones and drain the ancient lakes. To search for my likeness in a handful of dust. To add serpent-venom to wine—all part of our agreement. You are multiplying the silence that seeps ever-inward, scoring my insides. Tonight, I stack distance, balance time, hide away our memories: you will stop by to check on my progress. I'm almost liquid / with fear.

Transitive relocation centre; filmy façade; you take my last traces, bury them

Mar 2006
May 2012
July 2013
Feb-May 2014

Michelle Greenblatt

Tiniest, final perfection.

Now I would give a thousand furlongs of sea for an acre of barren ground...The wills above be done, but I would fain die a dry death.

> William Shakespeare
> *The Tempest*
> Act I, Scene i. *ll.* 62-64

The alkali tide blind-tosses me along its celestial riddle of waves. Each morning I cross the rickety bridge to the star-scorched quarry where, after falling, they transform, embers to earth. This is when I try to become young again. I begin every day in the smoke-filled meadows, gathering the liquid ribbons of Shannon's sapphire songs and wind them into garlands which dissolve whenever I remember her / discarded on the porch; they vanish when I think her name. But the ocean hums her forgotten songs; it sings her back to me: I remember each of her pale, perfect features down to the tiniest, final perfection.

Grant me just one vision, O enchanted prescription, her heroin hips and lips and eyes

Mar-Apr 2006
May 2012
July 2013
Feb-May 2014

The smallest of sighs.

O churl! drunk all, and left no friendly drop
To help me after? I will kiss thy lips;
Haply some poison yet doth hang on them,
To make die with a restorative.

> William Shakespeare
> *Romeo and Juliet*
> Act IV, Scene iv. ll. 3125-3128

Black henbane dyes the honey I'm forced to mix with the toxicant I stir into the black-currant wine, its heady bouquet the perfect disguise. You watch me as my lover drinks your deathbrew. Long ago, I figured your age by the half-life of the drugs destroying your insides. All the while, you try to teach me to keep my temper; you tell me not to strike at the prison walls. I've remained motionless today—here, her scent on you still fresh as flowers, I slide the knife between your shoulderblades. You betray the silence with the smallest of sighs.

The morning heat swells to noontime, I root myself out of the ground, your final breath's still sweet on my smiling cheek

> Mar 2006
> May 2012
> Mar-May 2014

Michelle Greenblatt

Calling down an avalanche.

> *Have not to do with him, beware of him:*
> *Sin, death, and hell have set their marks on him,*
> *And all their ministers attend on him.*
>
> > William Shakespeare
> > *Richard III*
> > Act I, Scene iii. ll. 291-293

Clenched in your fist is the avalanche you'll whisper down when I no provide you pleasure. I am biding my time, biding my time, trying to summon a warring rockslide. I exist in a perpetual state of asphyxiation. Your voice, curved as a kama, informs me that you are my home now—tenderness and brutality balanced against the self-sharpening edge of your blade. When you release my hand, I pick out sharded bits of glass. Light inhales the ashes of nighttime, consuming the shadows you leave behind. An invisible metronome is tick tick ticking away the seconds I have left until you decide my time / of death, calling down an avalanche.

Death sings across a selenocentric wire; no time left to start a stopgap fire; every night you festoon me with silk, ready to be set aflame...and one night soon you will douse me in gasoline

Mar 2006
May 2012
Mar-May 2014

The day you carved me into concentric circles.

The day you carved me into concentric circles, I chose to laugh instead of die. Since that day, I've been acutely aware of the actions I take, of all the ways you have changed me. When I breathe, I can feel the air in my lungs catch, snaring on my ribcage. The only evidence of violence I haven't amputated are the tears in the clothing I wore that day—I can't make myself throw them away. Now I watch you through nighttime's windowpane, tying gasoline-soaked rags around my effigy. I hold my pill-bottles in my scarred hands: one to make me smaller, ten to make taller, a hundred to make me sleep

Evidence of breathlessness, kerosene, eternity

Mar-Apr 2006
May 2012
July 2013
Mar-May 2014

Michelle Greenblatt

Ice blossoms on the snowfield.

thorns. Back at the rusted-open gate the gun-man waits, painting a smile on his hard, blank face. He crouches near the place where I become ice blossoms on the snowfield, folding and unfolding on the changing of the hour. Now Aidan and I are old again. What he knew of me was only a few coats of paint, and he scraped those away with a razorblade.

Frozen home, blackened roads, a spent casing hidden in blue-gold stones

Mar-Apr 2006
May 2012
Mar-May 2014

Struggle and flight.

For Kyle, the perfect mirror

Staring into the treacherous liquid-silver of your mirror, its depths slippery and shifting, I fall through the lightning-cracked blue of my eyes and plummet into the past. Tripping down the long, empty halls of memory, I recall being a child, before I'd learned to hate my face. Now mirrors seem the epitome of black magic to me. I'd imagine vats of molten glass, poured in layers of viscous argentate cooling into sheets of thick, reflective lacquer. I gaze into the high gloss of the gleaming looking-glass until my vision blurs. Upon its final trick of transformation, I am made / to crawl through a dilated-black portal, passing through an odyssey of smashed windowglass that displays the shattered pieces of my sharded face. I burn / a hole through time with my kiss, festoon my memories to your lips. To escape from your darkling kingdom, I must travel the most arduous paths. I trudge through the black waters of the contraband river, carrying years of secrets in my clenched fists. One day, I will wake to an aureate world, foreknown to warmth.

Stimulus mounds; slit-open clouds; the clocks on the rooftops tick, *time is telling*

Mar-Apr 2006
May 2012
Apr-Aug 2014

Michelle Greenblatt

Six years into my posthumous life.

What wafts in from the cave is not smoke from that slab / of a sleeping girl he keeps captive and burning, lying on the marble. Sunday after Sunday, we labor in our prisons with old faces, tired whispers, our same names. Six years into my posthumous life, I am older than ever before. I can't stop struggling against the hill's hanging relief; I can't make myself believe the ropes aren't as fragile as old ivy, ready to break over the infinite / abyss. In the sunken lanes where I sleep, the breeze hardens, condensing into a cold, bone-fingered wind. It shrieks my secrets to the sky and smudges the scenery, smearing it into the bracken, clotted with rotten leaves. Sour marshland, tainted water, dying trees. No matter, I'm little more than a swollen statistic now: I've bent your life; you've broken mine. The plethora of multicolored roads that lead home are lost to me. The rest is redundant.

Eyelash wish, the victim's kiss, bloodstripe on the finger morphs into warpaint on the face

Mar 2006
May 2012
Apr-Aug 2014

A posteriori.

Prismed glass scatters the haloed rays of aureate light into flimsy-ribboned rainbows. One more brain:storm from the curdled clouds, one more feathered vision to conceal the avalanche made to drag me back through the shadows / to you. At home with Kyle tonight, I skate over fat crusty ridges of ice. Tossed by a child, a penny skitters across the lake's surface. I wonder what she has wished for. My *a priori* detectors tremor; your gag of dreams forbids me to speak.

Retina rot; forget-me-not; after the fact / of you, brilliance turns sourblack

Mar 2006
May 2012
Aug-Sept 2014

Michelle Greenblatt

The question of thrown stones.

Thy broken faith hath made a prey for worms.
What canst thy swear by now?

        William Shakespeare
        Richard III
        Act V, Scene iv. ll. 386-887

Your final face hangs, a veil over your previous one. The most important aspect of the question of thrown stones has left nothing but a bitter impression of your portioned exaggerations as an etching on every wall. The stones stare through me—they are just props, but don't touch them, it's bad to break things. Instant after instant drags us together, even as it tears us apart.

Ice-coated lament; grief-painted song; dear God, please help me: I was wrong, *I was wrong*

Mar-Apr 2006
May 2012
Apr-Aug 2014

Stone among stones.

A new god with narrow eyes looks down on me today. He fills my room with unbelievables. I'd reach for them, but they aren't mine to have: touching them invokes his wrath. On my pilgrimage I pass the sea, His liquid lexicon. And when I walk over hellish roads with a stiff back and bleeding heels, my mouth full of gristle and my lips cracked with salt, I do so because it pleases Him. I am always small-fingered, my eyes frosty hollows, my teeth chattering / glass. I chew the day's dirt, a stone among stones.

Sun-torment, storm warnings, scatterings of scorn

Mar-Apr 2006
May 2012
Aug-Sept 2014

Michelle Greenblatt

Imagelines.

> *I notice how*
> *all your word-*
> *plays, calculated ploys*
> *of the body, the witticisms*
> *of touch, are now*
> *attempts to keep me*
> *at a certain distance*
> *and (at length) avoid*
> *admitting I'm here.*
>
>   Margaret Atwood
>   "The Circle Game" part vi.

His is a fleshly faith. Minds and (s)words do not concern him. He shovels his mouth full of meat as I point out, *The lightning conductor is as much metaphor as the alembic.* His irises grow darker and his pupils widen while kaledocopic imagelines encircle him, lighting up the circuits of his mind. He sucks the slit stems of flowers. He holds our hours in his hands.

Lightning seed; slab of meat; infinite, circulatory sea

Mar 2006
May 2012
Aug-Sept 2014

Water's desolate edge.

At the water's desolate edge where sun breaks into glints of light, I pick a jagged bit of mirrorglass out from between my teeth. Wingspan shrieks toward surrounded sound, a better way than the personified road we're traveling down. Still, I must find your face among the *acqua alta* while the tidal piranhas nibble at my gut with their brutal rows of jagged teeth. Your eyes are bloody lemons; the slit shadows are sky-green.

Trial and error, matchstick and machine, Magyar cave to pave

Mar 2006
May 2012
Aug-Sept 2014

Michelle Greenblatt

Filled with winter.

I fine-tune sentences into parallel structures because I am filled with winter. I have a secret so sad and filthy, no one wants to play with me. Of course I am here—I have to be. I kneel in the imperial tide that hopes to drag me out by my feet and drown me. I am assaulted by your falsetto dreams; their sharp sudden redness perforates me. Damaged light leaks in, makes want to call this "the edge". Even the sun is wet these days. The infected landscape tells me I'm lost again as I walk through a series of colors that dissolve into salt-cracked boundaries.

Navigation: nightly; my hands are empty; every truth spat out with bracken and bile

Mar-Apr 2006
May 2012
Aug-Sept 2014

A sufficient distance.

The canals and pits talk amongst themselves about the stringing and unstringing of paradoxes by hand. When they look up, they remember nothing but diagrams in thicket / form. They wonder: confronted with the knowledge that she tastes like dirty ice, how long can the girl stay? Clandestine stars gather 'round the moon's false glow. Hell is *not* imageless. How far, *how sufficiently far* must one surface-nerve travel along the ragged sieve of sun before she is finally found?

Soil, wrought wire, certainty-fire

Mar-Apr 2006
May 2012
Sept 2014

Michelle Greenblatt

Mo(u)rning announcements.

> *I took him for the plainest harmless creature*
> *That breathed upon this earth a Christian;*
> *Made him my book wherein my soul recorded*
> *The history of all her secret thoughts*
>
> William Shakespeare
> *Richard III*
> Act III, Scene v. ll. 2095-2098

Living spaces draw back their limbs at his mo(u)rning announcements. A universe flares up in my belly, strewing ashes and seeds about. I fall from an empty womb, a ransacked tomb, a hollow space in an infinitely-expanding hole. His stories forever publish my mind, my body. In the forest, in the shower stalls, in the bombed-out parts of me, each sparking candle is a reminder, a reminder, a reminder: he will neon himself like a dark star and play my black cloud until I rain again.

Buried din, coal and scrim, locked door on the 13th floor

Mar-Apr 2006
May 2012
Aug-Sept 2014

Color of crying.

Lead me from death to life, from falsehood to truth
Lead me from despair to hope.

>Satish Kumar
>"Prayer for Peace"

Barricaded door I've scratched at before. I torch the gauze on my body, throw topaz at the windows, listen to the sounds of the storm. The glazed path sobs, slick narrow noises the color of crying. I unfold and refold the note you left me, speaking of downed cities, drowned consciences. My laughter comes unpinned like hair in the wind and whips across my face, a wrathful hand. These days, I consist only of memories.

Lost time, botched rhyme, nothing anymore is mine

>Mar-Apr 2006
>May 2012
>Aug-Sept 2014

Michelle Greenblatt

Intent on haphazardness.

The man in red, intent on haphazardness. The girl in blue, hiding from him. The blur of brisk, parabolic air hovering between them smells like autumn in Fort Lauderdale. Makes her mind ripple, her lungs constrict. Under her feet, oak flooring. Her imagination in his fists.

Yellow-spring lash of memories, insomniac grip, a fit to follow / violence

Mar-Apr 2006
May 2012
Aug-Sept 2014

Missing.

The theoretical word is a handful of flares not yet shot into the sky, releasing its fiery sparks into galactic black. Nobody has spoken or thought this possible word. There is no memory of its syllabic mystery on a dead man's lips; the wind that confuses will keep on confusing all unspoken possibilities. Aware of my unawareness, I search daily in my simulacra of reality for this word, but can't find it. It is the word that waits for the end of the world: it will only be spoken to the void.

Salt-sea on thirst-cracked lips, smoke signals and mirror-tricks, the search for the face of death fails again

Mar-Apr 2006
May 2012
Sept 2014

Michelle Greenblatt

Press through panic.

> *...Or if she be accused in true report,*
> *Bear with her weakness, which, I think proceeds*
> *From wayward sickness.*
>
> >William Shakespeare
> >*Richard III*
> >Act I, Scene iii. ll. 27-29

I float my pattern on the floor, watching its deepening eddies of white. Above, the darkness; below, the fish / drowning on our windowsills. I press through panic: he as he was, he as he is. He slathers his hands in the primordial ooze seething from the ancient aqueducts. Open one door, a thousand others close. Nothing is added—so much is taken away.

Madness and her teeth, my hysterical stare, his red balloon winking in the searing noontime glare

Mar-Apr 2006
May 2012
Sept 2014

Midnight and mud.

My life has crept so long on a broken wing
Through cells of madness, haunts of horror and fear
That I come to be grateful at last for a little thing.

    Alfred, Lord Tennyson
    "Maud" pt. 2, sect. 6, st. II

There is a southern bludgeoning of road that pounds through the Everglades in a zigzagging pattern; it leads to my home. Quickly, take me there: the wind is giggling again. I will go to my bed. I will lie there quietly. I won't ask for food I won't ask for water I won't ask for a name. If you'd like to know, I will tell you why you must never climb down the black ladder—only stay, stay with me. I will tell you about Adam Ant and how he eats his girls; I won't complain of ruined memorabilia or tell you what it feels like to taste midnight and mud each time I get lost in the devilwood forest. Help me press through this / panic and I will never ever bend shadows or truth the way he taught me to.

Disaster engenders disaster, ruin reproduces ruin, despair recreates despair

Mar 2006
May 2012
Sept 2014

Michelle Greenblatt

Clotted wisdom.

The sharp intonations of vanishing water bounce perilously off the veil of bogscrapings he drapes over the hallucinations he calls / his visions. As shamanistic seer, he finds hidden wisdom in strange places—as in, wisdom hoarded in washroom cupboards, wisdom curdled in unwashed dishes, wisdom clotted in kitchen drains. The world is shrinking. He orders his followers, *Gather at the place where central ventilation is observed. We shall have a holocaust: I'll make rhythmical representation render the wretched unto ash, then throw my desire back until the seeds I have planted bear first fruit.*

Young, hunger-lean lips will always whisper magic words; a strained and manic expansion of the oldest prayers; ancient ears will hear no water-starved incantations

Mar 2006
May 2012
Sept 2014

Employ then empty.

You call these motions I go through "the process of recovery" as if I gather disordered data and not my busted-up life. Meanwhile, you cast aside all restrictions for yourself, ransack the emergency supplies, employ then empty the sealed aquifers of language reserved for catastrophe. You hunt the weak and injured for sport as well as for supper: you've taught your hounds to track them to slaughter by following their acrid odor: a sick, acidic smell, part glandular, skunky and strong; part inside of a shredded stomach: the scent of their fear. Through preparation and slow-sweep surveillance, one can be ready for much.

Law and order, intoxication by lottery, malice required to rule

Mar-Apr 2006
May 2012
Sept 2014

Michelle Greenblatt

And *how does that make you feel?*

Violence returns (as it is wont to do) on a calm golden day during mid-spring. Mother forces me into therapy again. I lash out with porcelain nails and a cigarette, drawing blood from an arm (I don't know whose) while the lake flips so that bottom-up becomes as murky as my mind. Seething, *I could kill, I could kill*. A few careless flicks of a razor to the wrist—I could kill myself, Mother. *That's* how this makes me feel.

Quiescent tide; amidst the slaughter, conquered daughter; bitter end to your pretty girl

Mar-Apr 2006
May 2012
Sept 2014

Softly, softly.

Ablaze with celestial light, he arrives as though riding a hijacked dream. Softly, softly, he touches her face. The certainty of the moment breaks / through her mangled existence, shattering her garments of ice. Embracing, they kiss passionately. This breakneck bliss feathers the blossoming poppies against the gentle sunlight streaming between the branches of the sentinel trees. Once again, she is thunder / struck by him, the atom-splitting, lightning-force of his existence—hotter than any sun—flowing right / beneath his skin. Though taken / aback by his unswerving intent to find another face and a different name for her, she abandons herself to his sure current, the fiery scansions running through him.

Confusion, newness, love arranges sudden changes again

Mar 2006
May 2012
Sept 2014

Michelle Greenblatt

After the holocaust.

I stroll through the blended sounds amid this blurred scenery; I search for syllables to describe the moon, arranged in skewed, semi-circular slices. An early winter and the north-easterly winds have me / shivering. I set fire to my memory; I funnel color after color, shape after shape into the flames. After the holocaust / eradicates the daylight, the ashy wind seethes its farewells, walling all words into and around seared sound. I screen my stored images for a single glimpse of you, but my visions are depleted, diminished, deformed. The worry splits my memories—once fixed as a steady heartbeat—into slit meiotic strips.

Phantom sounds, water resounds, repetition of over and over again

Mar-Apr 2006
May 2012
Sept 2014

Highlighter fluid and water.

> *Decline all this, and see what now thou art:*
> *For happy wife, a most distressed widow;*
> *For joyful mother, one that wails the name;*
> *For queen, a very caitiff crown'd with care;*
> *For one being sued to, one that humbly sues;*
> *For one that scorn'd at me, now scorn'd of me;*
> *For one being fear'd of all, now fearing one;*
> *For one commanding all, obey'd of none.*
>
>   William Shakespeare
>   *Richard III*
>   Act IV, Scene iv. ll. 2892-2899

After you stole the engagement ring you gave to me, you submerged it in a glass of sour milk, thinking it hidden within the creamclotted liquid beneath its moldblue skin. In a drunken moment of post-coital weakness, you whispered your glee to your fuck of the week across red satin sheets, admitting you still dream of me, my weeping face peering through old Sambuca bottles filled with highlighter fluid and water. Meanwhile, my efforts to climb inside the wolf's world fails: I am trapped within this shameful sheepskin; the sizeable swamp I live in keeps shrinking. Among these pages, my stunted poetry unmakes me with its metaphors. I want your eyes, your lips, your heart / trapped within my crushing hands.

Smashed ashtray; brute light; this old bite, festering, festering...

                                                        Mar-Apr 2006
                                                          May 2012
                                                      Aug-Sept 2014

Michelle Greenblatt

All life's discolorations.

I have been bent since I was ten and broken since I was seventeen, snapped in half by the one who swore he loved me best and most and always. Star-smashed and sky-scattered, suspended in an eye-gleam full of spinal fluid and a mouthful of cord blood, I wander in and out of traffic. The snakespiral of shock locked in my mind begins to uncoil. My eyes fly open, jerking me out of the torment of my dreamriver, commencing the daily exchange: that sleeping nightmare for this waking one. Dawn dangles just over the horizon, scorching and malignant. All my life's discolorations bleed.

Promises and atrocities, no higher authority, my plethoric stores of insanity

Mar-Apr 2006
May 2012
Aug-Sept 2014

Steel smiles in time.

His murderous hands assail infinity. His reptilian tongue, his cold heart and frigid lips denounce her, vow never / again to be moved by her. He will keep her here, in this perfect little prison, disguised as a gilded palace; he will never let her up from his procrustean bed. *I get my facelessness from you*, she said to him, her version of a curse. He showed her his teeth. But now her eyes—fixed and horrified—can find him in any mirror. He moves through the castle armed only with anonymity, which is no defense against atrocity, as every glass surface here knows. The stares of the statues all become steel smiles in time.

Detainment, declension, a plethora of mirrors and malice aforethought

Mar 2006
May 2012
Aug-Sept 2014

Michelle Greenblatt

The splitting tissues of time.

And Juliet bleeding, warm, and newly dead,
Who here hath lain these two days buried.

        William Shakespeare
        Romeo and Juliet
        Act V, Scene iii. ll. 3144-3145

The secret summer we hid our honeysuckle on into evening, the shivering milk of the frail young flowers was warm on the west door of the splitting tissues of time. I chew the rinds of the moon's slowly dwindling seedy orbit. The sea is hot and shallow, wears her final face. Too deep for the glitter-slicked shouts to carry much sound in their blue brilliance, for the deviltrees to sprawl in later decadence, for the point-blank, sullen look to behave straightways on my face. The clangorous birds open their talons, trying to clutch sky. They fly over the beheaded mountains, ripping upward with their unearthly cries. I knife open a river. I stand a long while like a woman awakening.

Without world; upon solid sound; mirrors only mirrors, after all

                                                                  Mar 2006
                                                                 Sept 2014

Persephone's blood.

> *At evening, casual flocks of pigeons make*
> *Ambiguous undulations as they sink,*
> *Downward to darkness, on extended wings.*
>
> > Walt Whitman
> > "Sunday Morning"

She curves the blade downward toward darkness; she fine-tunes the hours but the muteness of his minutes is fresh. She looks at me and says, *Today is one of those days I would prophesy something explicit, but awash in the wrong life*. The one she runs from told her she should dwell only in dark places. Offshore, he gains power. She breaks a glance free from his hypnotic poison and dives, aslant, away from what he says. At first she is overly cautious, but she knows that which is dead does not always stay that way.

Midnight warning, Persephone's blood as razorpaint, five o'clock folly—pure and holy were those days

Mar-Apr 2006
Sept 2014

Michelle Greenblatt

Almost April.

Sin like smoke in the city streets, ambulance sirens pick up its sound, throwing it round and round in spiny red circles. March again. Almost April. I stroll on the walkway that winds through my front yard. I take gracious steps, consider the grass, the greenery, always the same-ghost figures wrapped around each tree, watching me smoke menthol cigarettes over the years. There is change in all things, all things except me.

Ampler skyline, magic trace, dusk erases all but this

Mar-Apr 2006
Sept 2014

Burns another spoon.

The water is wide, I can-not cross o'er.
And neither have I the wings to fly.

"The Water Is Wide"
English fok song

She appears as I stare at the smoldering moon. She scratches at my window; her wingbones look nothing like a warrior's. She listens for rain, a thin vapor above her. It swaddles her in its wet misery. She burns another spoon.

Flash of fate, husk of hate, eventual surrender

Mar 2006
Sept 2014

Michelle Greenblatt

Darkening the West.

He cannot live, I hope; and must not die

> William Shakespeare
> *Richard III*
> Act I, Scene i. l. 152

The Prince straps on his Janus mask. His dark snake oozes in and out of her castle's crevices. Every slithering motion leaves a stone; each scores the moon. He befriends the massive shadow of the moon and strips the petals off the palace blossoms. He gathers fruit, crushing their ripeness between bare hands; their sticky nectar trickles down his track-marked arms. In the royal abattoir, he sacrifices oceans. These salty deeds stick to him. He extends his vast wings of wire. All the West darkens.

Scarlet streaks / twine through his every chord of fire; the conjured rain rips away her tarp; laughing, he mimes the futility of hope

Mar-Apr 2006
July-Sept 2014

Shorn-blue.

It's about to be early; she's about to be late. He has covered every shred of her / sexuality with sawdust; everything she says comes out her mouth in a comic strip balloon. The edges he once precisely tore are now ragged as her shorn-blue eyes. The pair are young, obsessive, terrified—how to describe these changelings' irises? Two stormblue fronts pinned against pale, stagnant sky.

Smack, shame me, something irrevocable takes place every ticktock second

Mar-Apr 2006
Sept 2014

Michelle Greenblatt

Code red.

> *The pungent oranges and bright, green wings*
> *Seem things in some procession of the dead,*
> *Winding across wide water, without sound.*
> *The day is like wide water, without sound,*
> *Stilled for the passing of her dreaming feet*
> *Over the seas, to silent Palestine,*
> *Dominion of the blood and sepulchre*
>
>   Walt Whitman
>   "Sunday Morning"

Home is where the white bridge spans April, the wide water at the sea's battered edge; where humidity consistently interrupts conversation; where the approaching light lacquers the core of the legend's cruelest stones. It's where you pound me into the sand of the little scarlet island for wanting for more. Now when I pass by your careful display of my skeletons, I don't have to force my gaze away. I hardly / ever complain. Dispose of me as you will...only spare me / this spider-webbed darkness which fissures into a trial of unendurable nights, then splits into furrows before finally flatlining.

Deepening red, day of the dead, smoldering feversky

Mar-Apr 2006
July-Sept 2014

Self-division.

I open my arms to receive the night and it devours me. During these fleeting, self-seeing moments, you will find me staring into the sky. 7:13 p.m.: I cross the street. I can barely see in front of me to stamp my damp footprints in the mud: a sign, any sign, that I have been here. When the minutes begin / to self-divide, I sense my love has wandered from me. I walk by the canal the workmen are digging parallel to my home and kick more dirt in the muddied waters. A memory of us re-invents itself, altering its textured borders to please me.

Ashen tree, lucent seeds, bundled brightness bears down

Mar-Apr 2006
July-Sept 2014

Michelle Greenblatt

He fell away.

for José Perez 8.29.1984-3.26.2006

Death's semantics rattle their cage-bars. Destined to fall, the drop raises its head, looks inside itself, then separates. The few clouds that carry the sky shake the rain / water free and depart. At 3:26 p.m., the remnants of fractured sky go dark. Only Kyle and I are left. Jose is "dead from asthma" (but it was heroin that stopped his heart). Through the sad miasma of our bitter cigarettes, we see a faceless man making furtive gestures. We follow him to the simmering edge of summer, where he suddenly disappears. You are still alive. I shake with relief.

Walk without moving; move without waking; in the middle of a phrase, he fell away

Mar 2006
Aug-Sept 2014

Celestial utterances.

Bettering thy loss makes the bad causer worse:
Revolving this will teach thee how to curse.

    William Shakespeare
    Richard III
    Act IV, Scene iv. *ll.* 2917-2918

The midday sun burns into my eyes, making reflecting pools of my pupils. I try to wipe your traces off my body, but your oily gaze leave black grease all over me. You teach the constellations to whisper curses, and other unholy things. I pour palpable principles over your head to anoint you. You slash the earth with your teeth, smiling muddily.

Marble shudder, bramblewood flutter, confluence of celestial utterances

Mar-Apr 2006
Aug-Sept 2014

Michelle Greenblatt

Where you will find us.

It's where the wooden bridge collapses and meets the water, where we are prone to landslides and their bruise-colored natures. It's where the skyflow is slow and leaks into containers we brought from our old home back when we were crazy winged things, and it's where the willows only grow around the abyssal edges. Form takes life and life takes form. Seaweed tangles around our ankles; unsteady apparitions take our hands and guide us to safer places. We dive over deserts and barren cliffs; we don't speak a word until we must...and then no word is spared.

Sutured symphony, querulous euphony, simple sounds uttered in speculative tones

Mar 2006
Aug-Sept 2014

Pitch.

I want to pick it up
in my hand
I want to peel the
skin off; I want
more to be said to me

        Margaret Atwood
        "Against Still Life"

The trees on the path down by the ditch softly molt their greenery. Invisible waves of neon song smooth me out, back and forth, back and forth, through nighttime's cage as the words on the page lift off rhythmically. The notes, measurement-shaped and column-carved to fit the vertical structure, are pitched from scream to silence, from spacelessness to labyrinth. What it says it is, is what it doesn't say, and it never speaks what it means.

Touch to taste, orb to race, hands as moon and stars

Mar-Apr 2006
Aug-Sept 2014

Michelle Greenblatt

Mouth to skin.

> *released*
> *from the lucidities of day*
> *when you are something I can*
> *trace a line around, with eyes*
>
> Margaret Atwood
> "Pre-Amphibian"

I snag you between my teeth, your skin soft as an infant's. At first you fight, then relent / against my curious tongue. This is how we begin: mouth to skin. Later on, in the same room, we talk philosophy: Anne Sexton, the 2nd Amendment, how to steal 10 seconds from a very strict clock. We bruise ourselves when we try to get comfortable, and relax only when we don't realize it...Now, to sleep. But I can't and you can't, so we bury seeds and we wait—patiently, we wait.

Today, any day, someday / is now

Mar-Apr 2006
Aug-Sept 2014

On black limbs.

A kiss for virgin lips. Masks with two faces stalk the halls in order to find the bodies; bodies on all fours stalk the halls in order to find the masks. One may remain motionless while moving through time's dark corridors in search of eyes, nails and finger-bones. One may attempt to plant roots or clots or sparks of light in captured skies, or to drink a world, a weapon, an incompleteness down. Rapid hands spread cold like an oilcloth over the narrowblack landscape. Heat's kiss transforms the roads into impassable alleys of measureless travel. Winter skitters away on black limbs.

Awareness, preparedness, homage to isolation's depravity

Mar-Apr 2006
Aug-Sept 2014

Michelle Greenblatt

Consecrated.

> *Things that, to hear them told, have made me tremble;*
> *And I will do it without fear or doubt,*
> *To live an unstain'd wife to my sweet love.*
>
> > William Shakespeare
> > *Romeo and Juliet*
> > Act IV, Scene i. ll. 2452-2454

Absent one, I hear you come / against the edges of ice breaking off into the swollen river. The whiplash days, long as years, shimmer mid-air before they slap across the neon rocks in waves. Before you come forth, know this: there is time within time for us—time without hours or burden or weight. I will take you past all forbidden doors and press your fingers to the roar of my pulse, my pulse. I will lay myself on the stone altar in the forest outside the profaned city, to be consecrated.

Faces to wear, freedoms to swear, cathartic words to utter

Mar-Apr 2006
Aug-Sept 2014

ASHES AND SEEDS

Repairing the black.

*I'd rather say
I like your
lean spine
or your eyebrows
or your shoes*

*but just by standing there and
being awkward*

you force me to speak

love.

>   Margaret Atwood
>   "Letters, Towards and Away," part iv.

In the borderland, my hands endlessly extend, presenting my desires. While I wait for your return to memory, I repair the black / gaps in the wounded trees. If I am still alive when you return, you will find me walking down the road that leads to your Fort Lauderdale home. Stay where you are: alight in the shadows of all those days / finally unchained.

Repose of prose, whiteness of wide water, presences aligned to end infinity

>   Mar-Apr 2006
>   Aug-Sept 2014

Michelle Greenblatt

Each perpetual pause.

> *The people who come here also*
> *flow: their bodies becoming*
> *nebulous, diffused, quietly*
> *spreading out into the air across*
> *these interstellar sidewalks*
>
> Margaret Atwood
> "A Place: Fragments," part iv

White shadows circle dark stones. The stones turn themselves over / to thought. Your tongue phosphoresces on the handful of kisses that I tossed you years ago. I close my eyes, watch our thoughts go by. They flare up and flare up and flare up. The sky wrinkles with delight; the unsummoned clouds make music of raindrops. I throw myself into the wind, bodiless for a second, in your presence with nothing less than fullness and abundance. No hour is the same hour: each perceptual pause holds eternity / in its power.

Center of marvels, case of clarity, the perpetual principles of a dream

Mar-Apr 2006
Aug-Sept 2014

Without the help of a ladder.

Here all year long I've kept my secrets. The eerie blossoming of flowers in winter frightened me every time their petals opened to scent the chill wind. This season, I climbed long, high miles over danger without the help of a ladder more times than I can count. I've huddled in trenches and hidden in trees 'til they tripped me, trapped me, threw me down; I've been twisted / beyond recognition and I remained that way, stuck in a sickening tangle of twisted limbs. I've fallen through the floors of dark, anonymous rooms; I've sat frozen in panic until I remembered to look up, then found a plump skyline full of wider wings than I have ever seen or dreamed. Whole worlds whip past me, beckoning. The only blood-borne cries I hear now have dimmed.

Eyes; throat; lips: exposed, mark the beginning of the first creation-kiss

Apr 2006
July 2013
Aug-Sept 2014

Special thanks to Pearl Goldman, Kyle Ramsay, Michael Patrick McClellan, and Jonathan Penton. You four are the best friends and editors anyone could ever hope for. Without your invaluable support, advice, inspiration and encouragement, publishing ASHES AND SEEDS would not have been possible. My thanks as well to Dr. Mark Scroggins, Dan Waber, Dr. John Childrey, and so many others for their inspiration and support. My gratitude to cover artists Stephen Harrison and Monika Mori | MOO.

Michelle Greenblatt

Excerpts from "Streaks of Scarlet: A Story in 100 Parts" were previously published in *Bone Orchard Poetry*.

"Catherine's Absence," "Atomic time.," "Songs of Elemental Change," "Shadows Turn Bright" (as untitled), "The (W)hole of the Unknown" (as "In Between the Closed Parentheses"), "My Light with Your Teeth," and "How We Died, All Those Times" were previously published in *Unlikely 2.0* and *Unlikely Stories: Episode IV*.

"Exsanguination.," "Against the grey.," "Almost liquid.," "Struggle and flight.," and "Where you will find us." were previously published in *Of/With*.

"Water's desolate edge.," "Mo(u)rning announcements." (as "Ashes and Seeds"), "Midnight and mud." (as "If You'd Like to Know"), "Softly, softly.," "After the holocaust." (as "Into and Around Better Sound"), "Steel smiles in time." (as "His Hands Assail Infinity"), and "Persephone's blood." (as "Downward toward Death") were previously published in *Otoliths*.

"A *posteriori*.," "On black limbs.," "Each perceptual pause." (as "The perpetual principles of a dream.") and "Without the help of a ladder." were previously published in *Femmewise Cat* (a division of *Clockwise Cat*)."

ASHES AND SEEDS

Michelle Greenblatt is the Poetry and Music Editor for *Unlikely Stories: Episode IV* and previously served as Co-Editor of Poetry for the now-defunct AND PER SE AND. A two-time Pushcart Prize nominee, she has been published in literary journals such as *Poetry Magazine, Sugar Mule, Free Verse, Altered Scale, Sawbuck, Hamilton Stone Review, Moria, Shampoo, Coconut Poetry, BlazeVOX, X-stream, Counterexample Poetics, Word for/Word,* and *Otoliths*. Her first solo book, *brain:storm*, was published by Anabasis Press. More recently, she has focused on collaborative works, such as *Ghazals* with Sheila E. Murphy (Cricket Press, 2007) and *Dark Hope* with Vernon Frazer (Argotist E-Books, 2011). She lives in South Florida with her beloved, Kyle.

Printed in Great Britain
by Amazon